A Picture Book of Cows

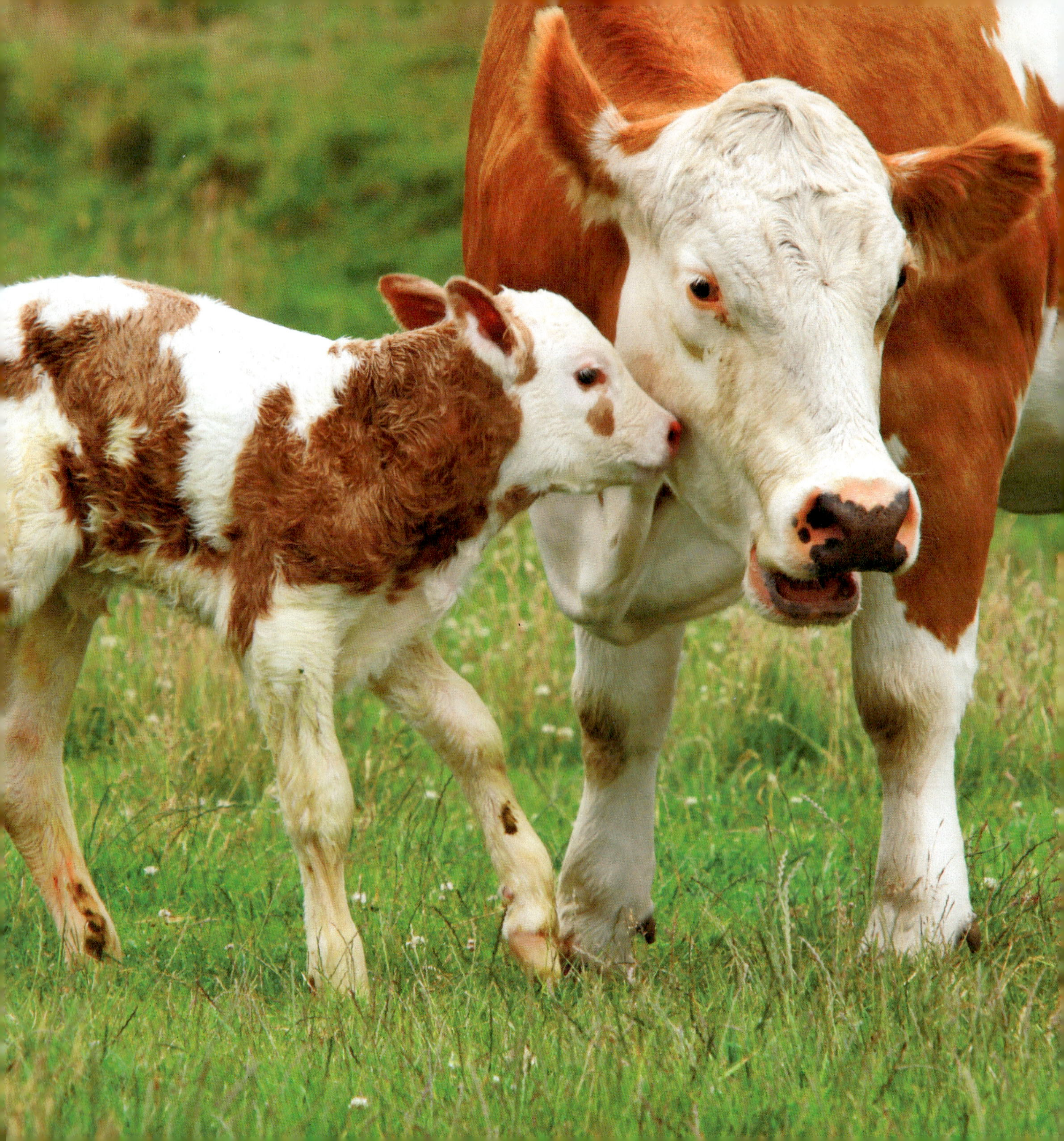

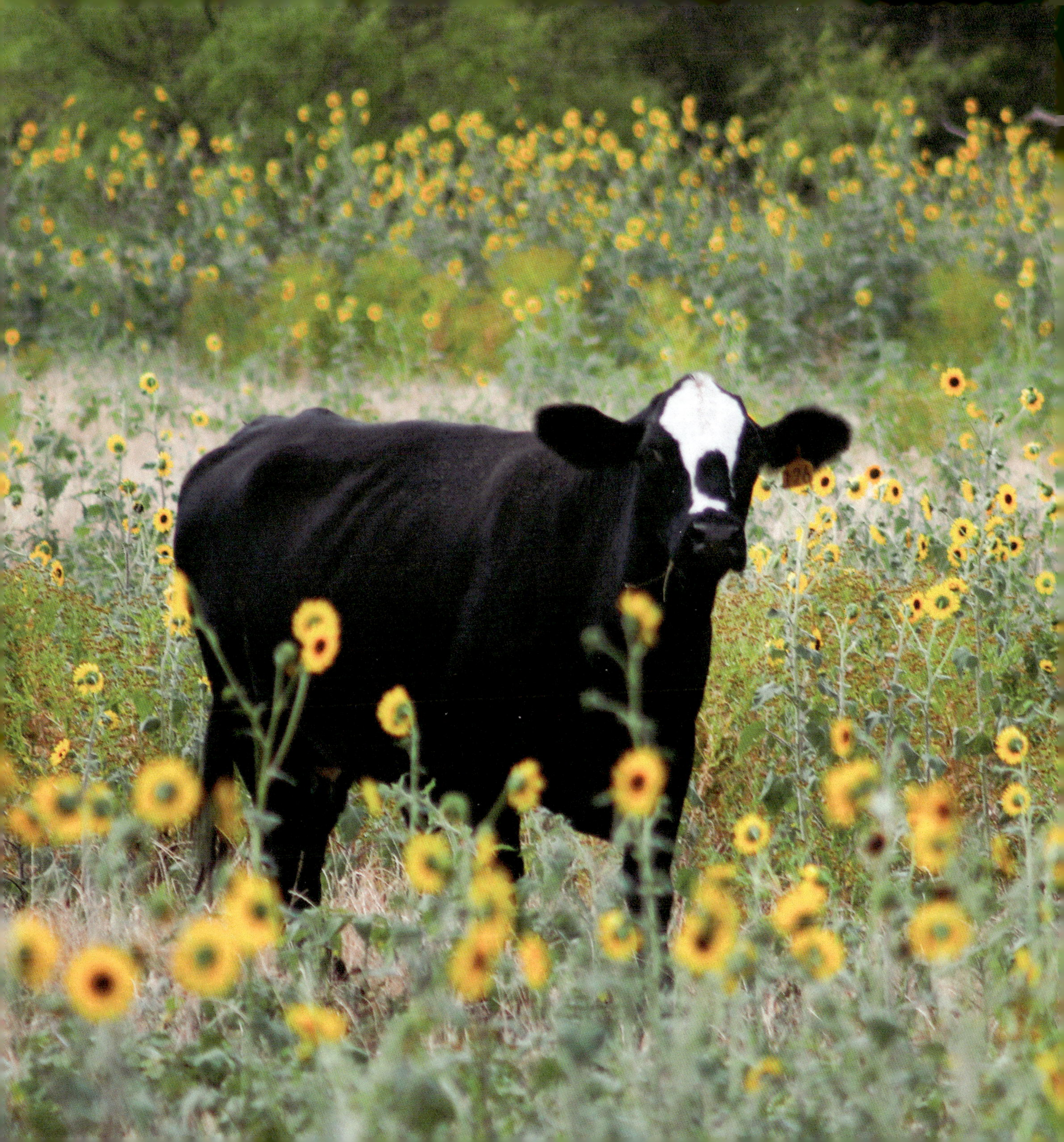

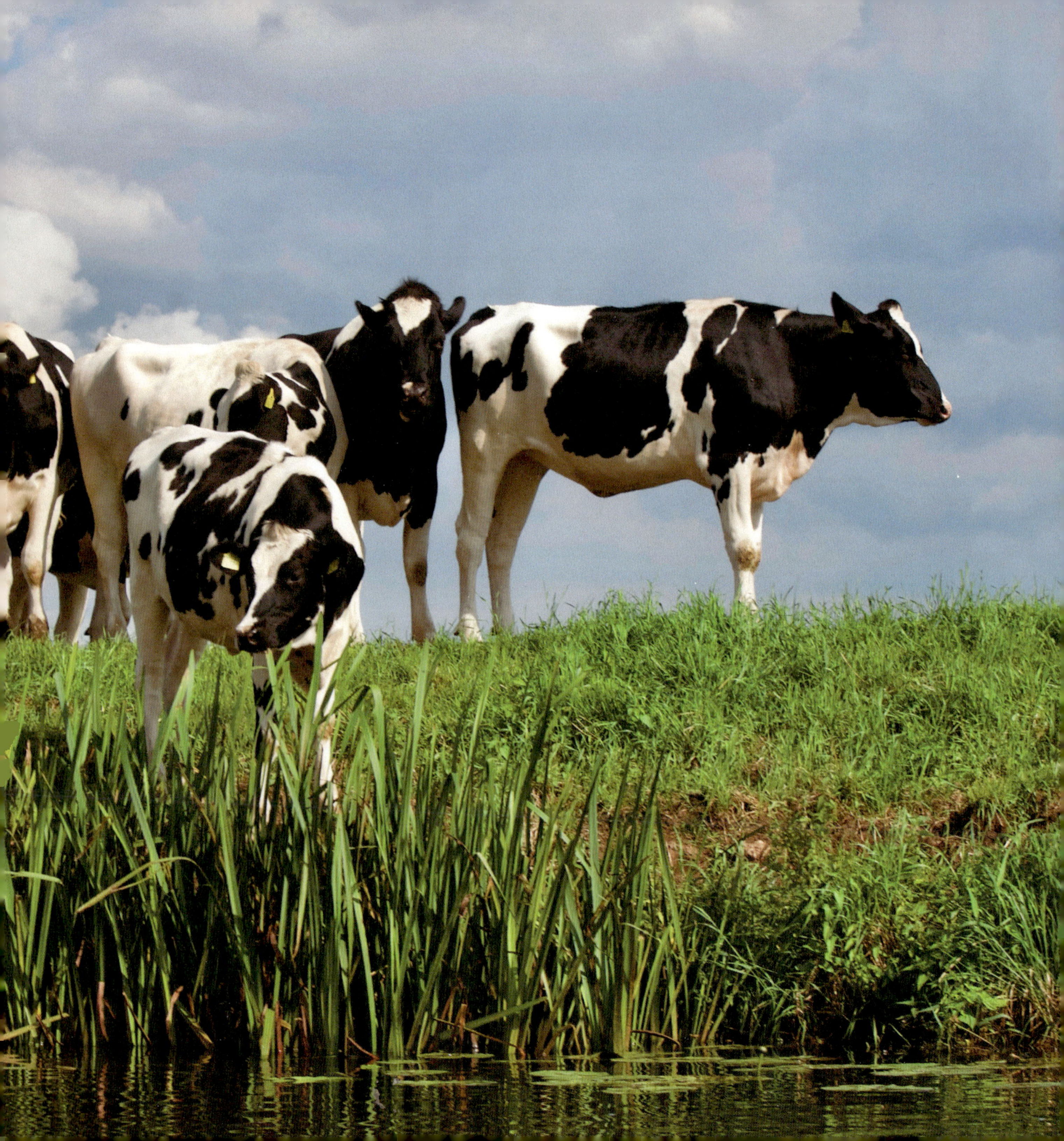

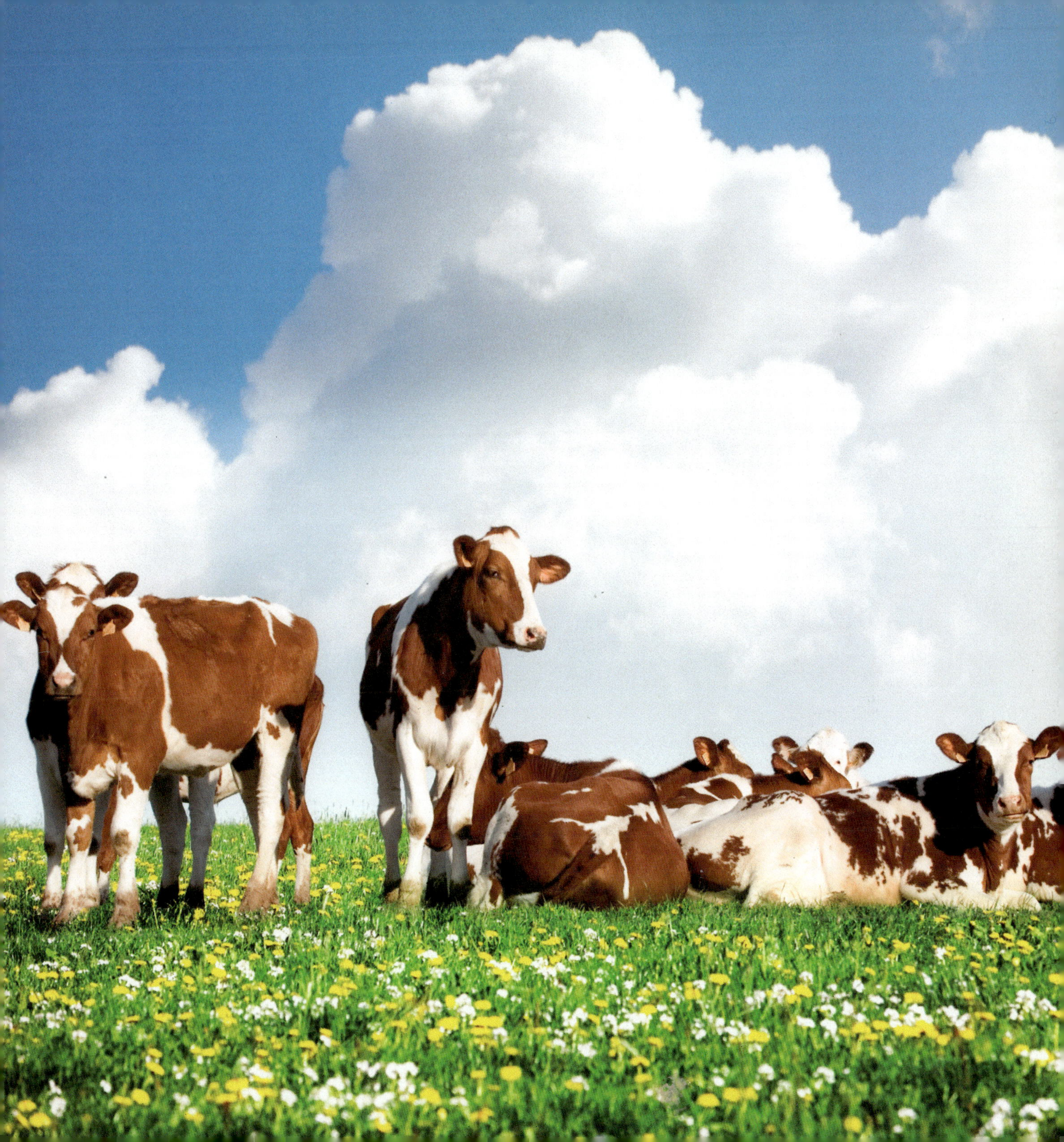

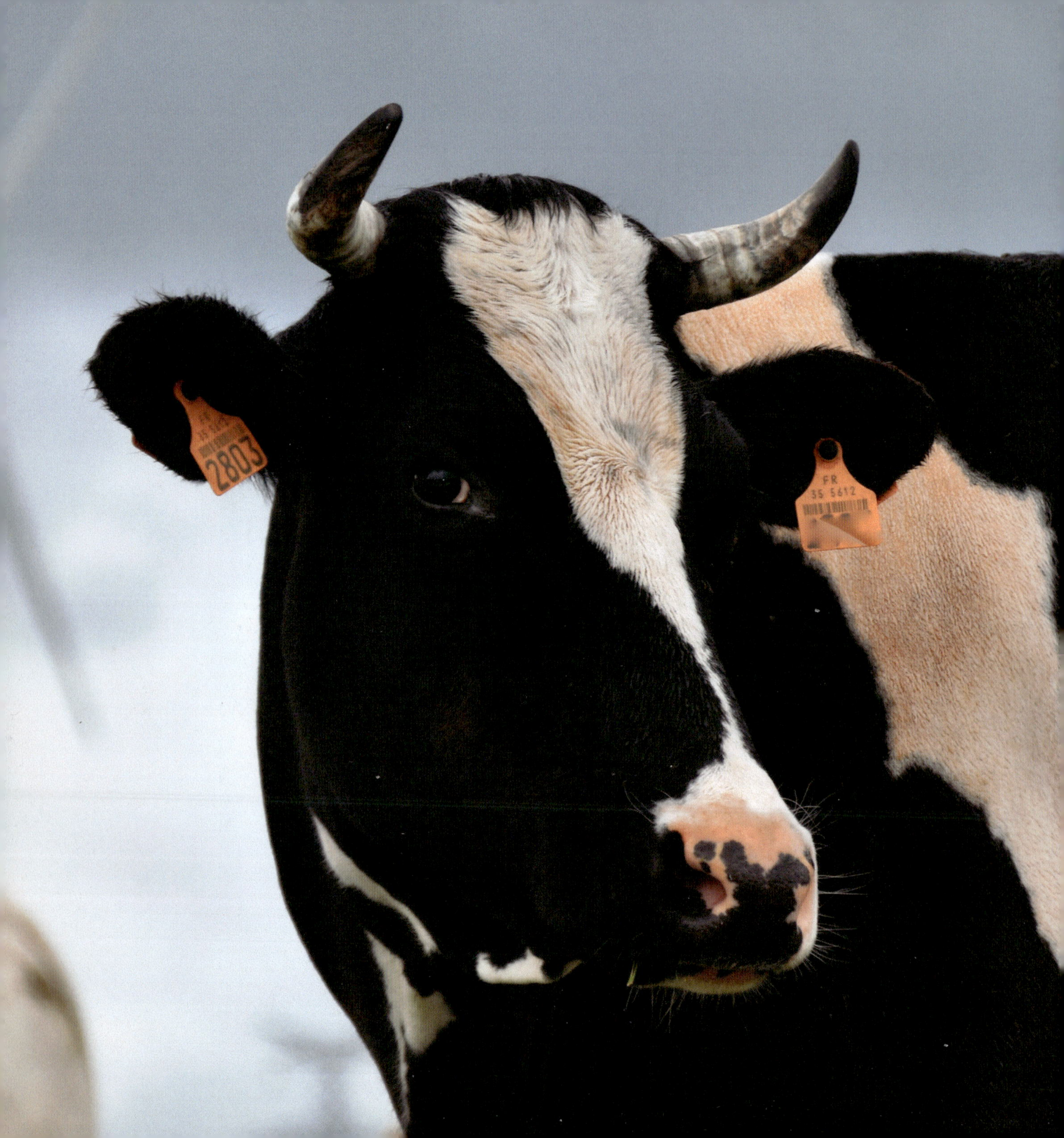
2803
FR
35 5612

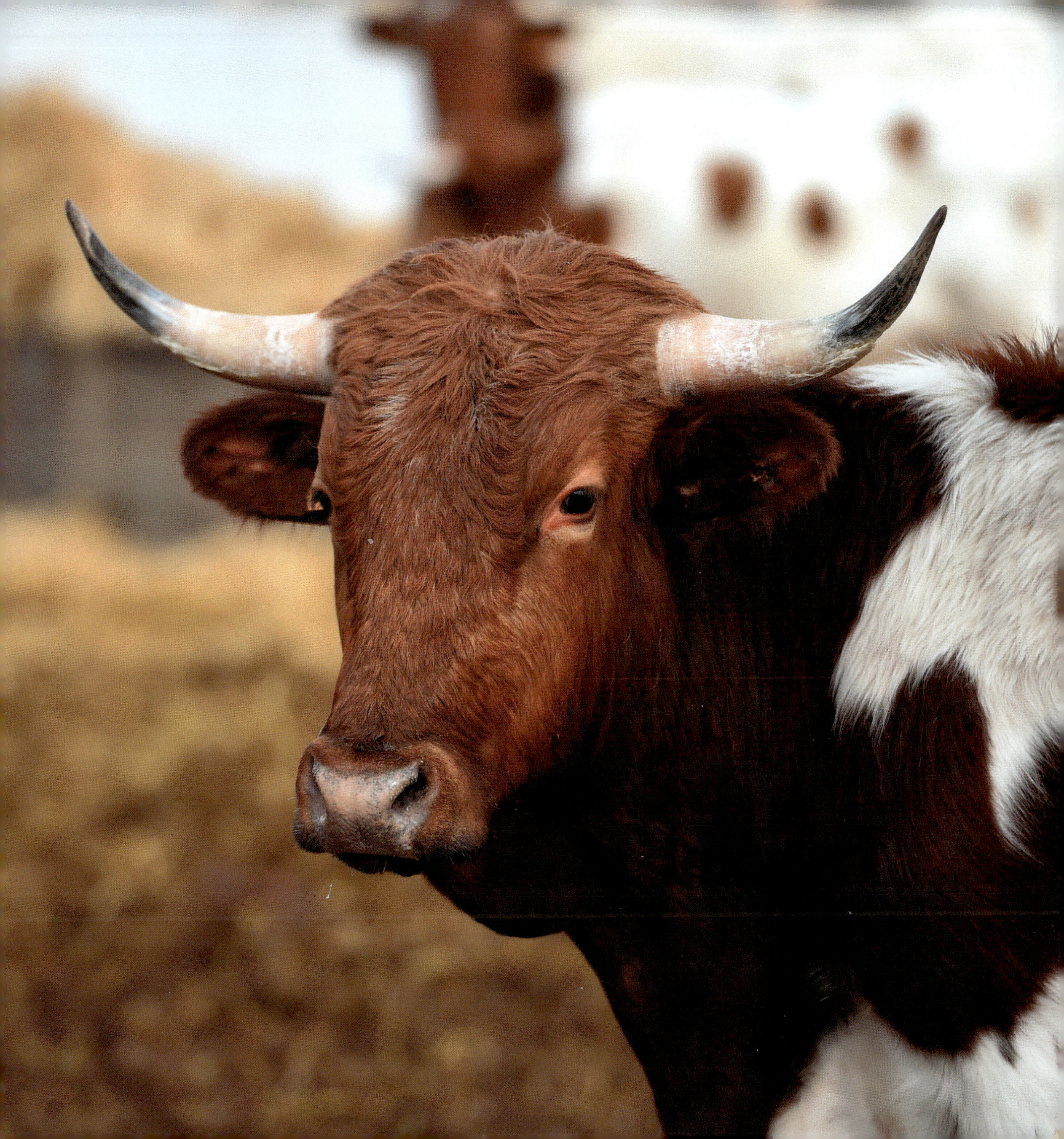

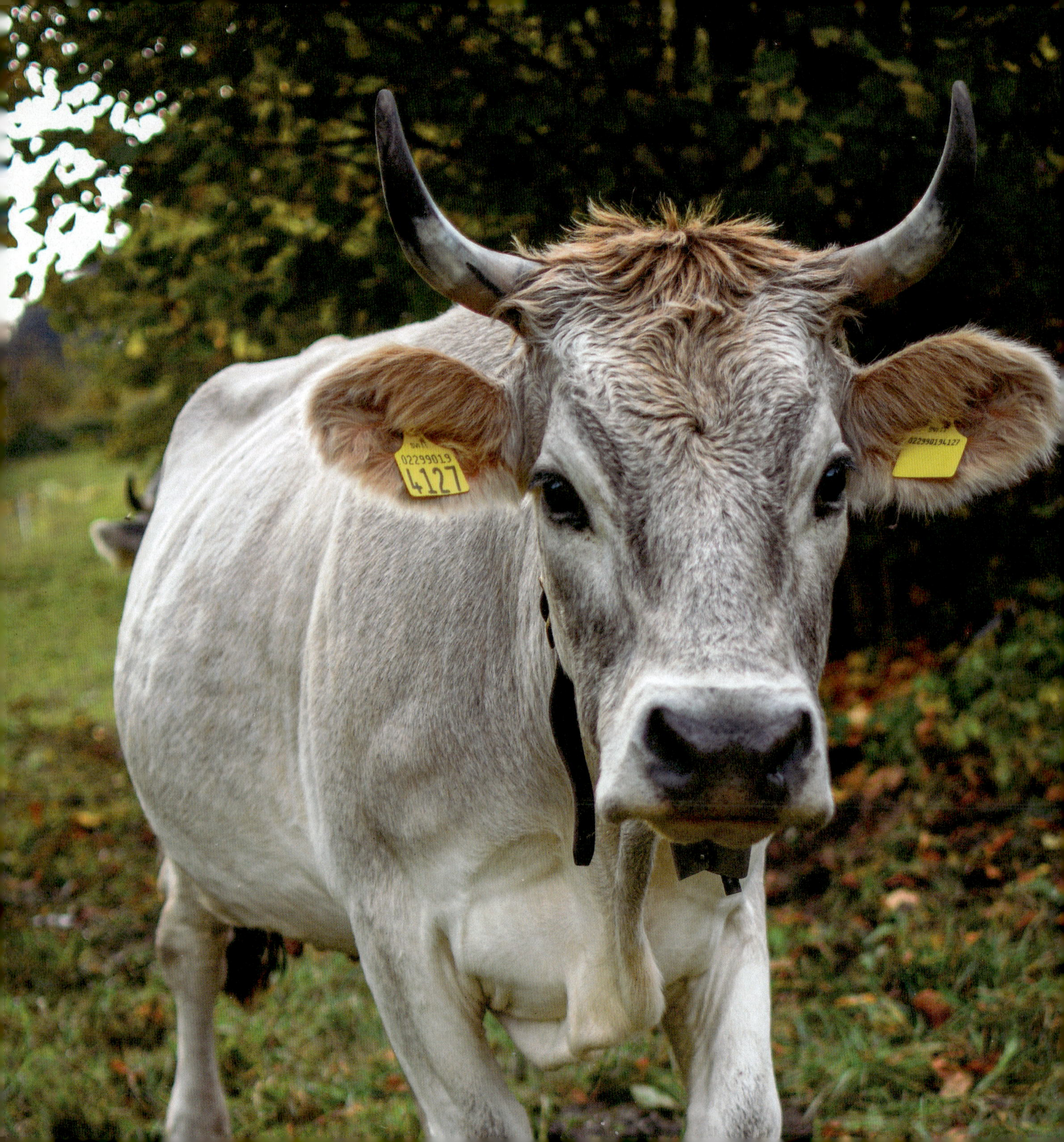
02299019
4127
02299019 4127

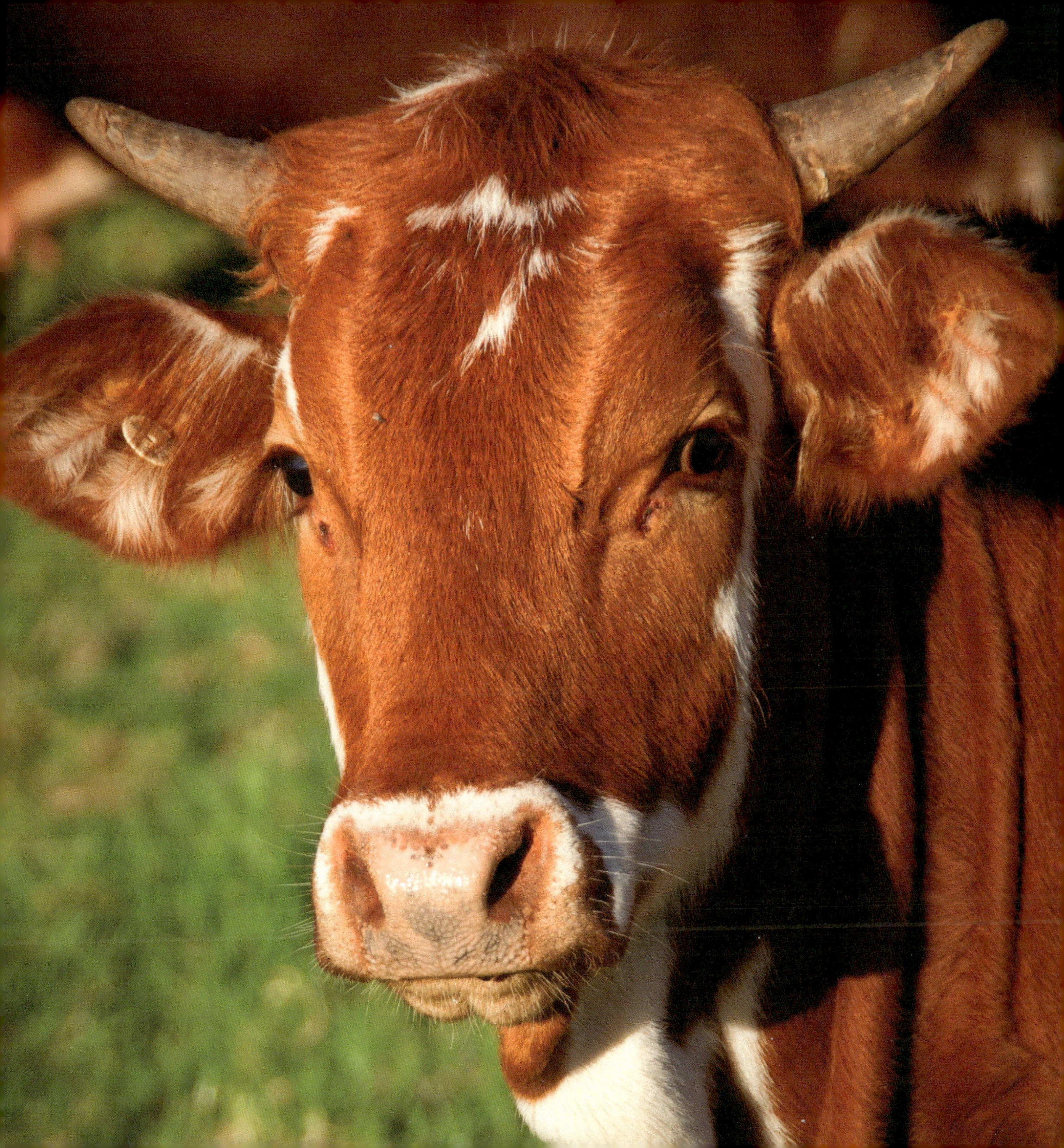

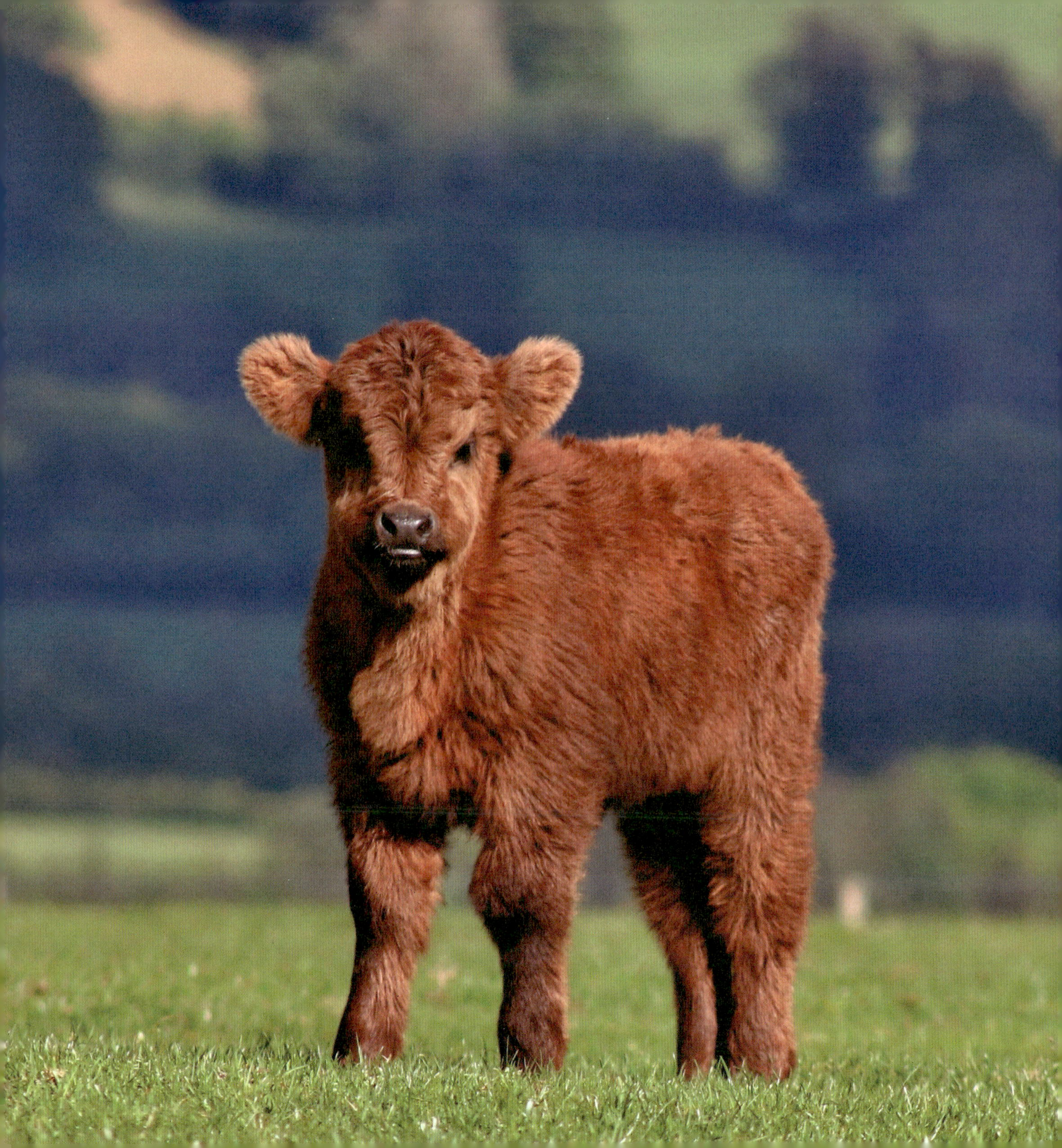

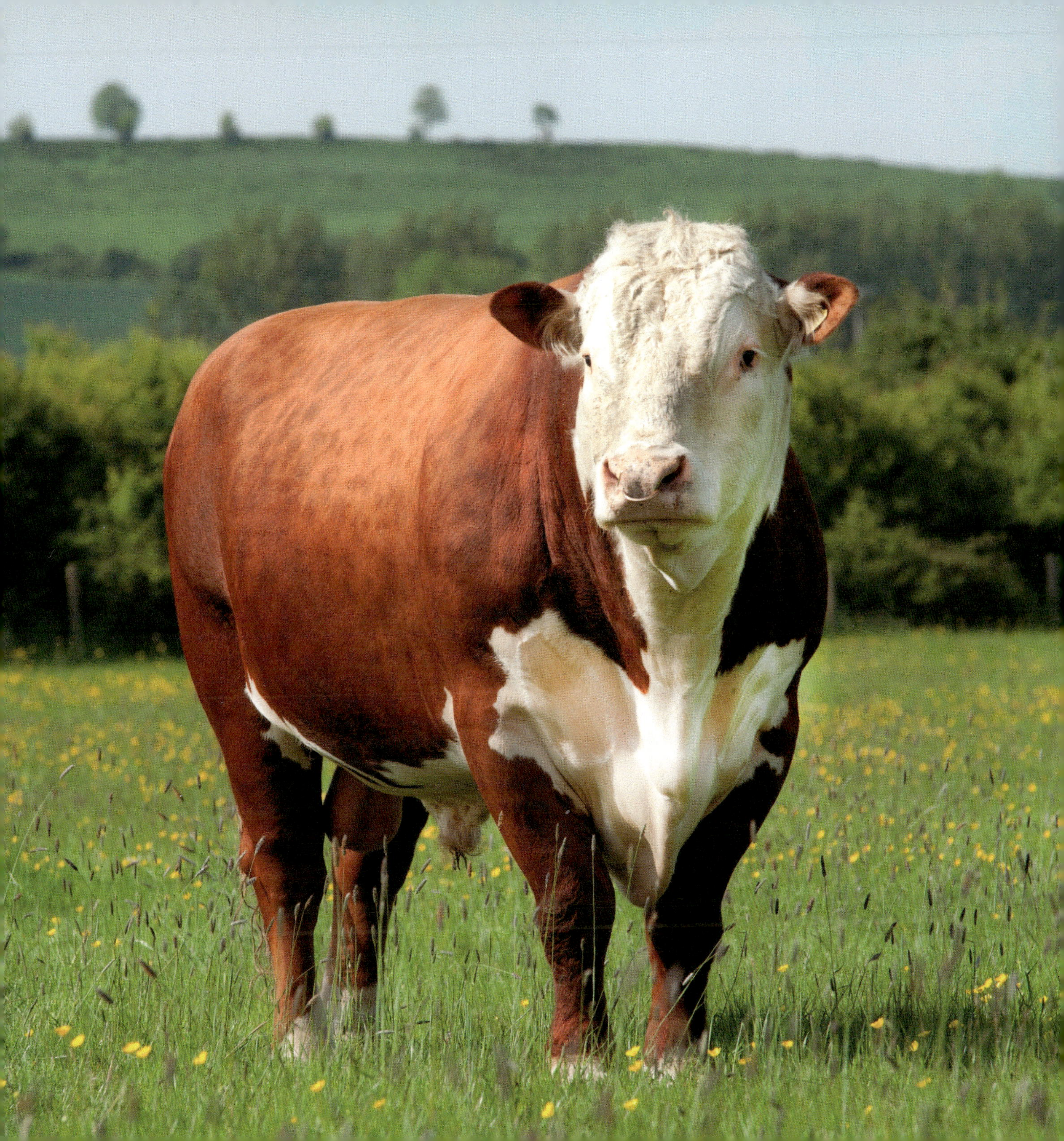

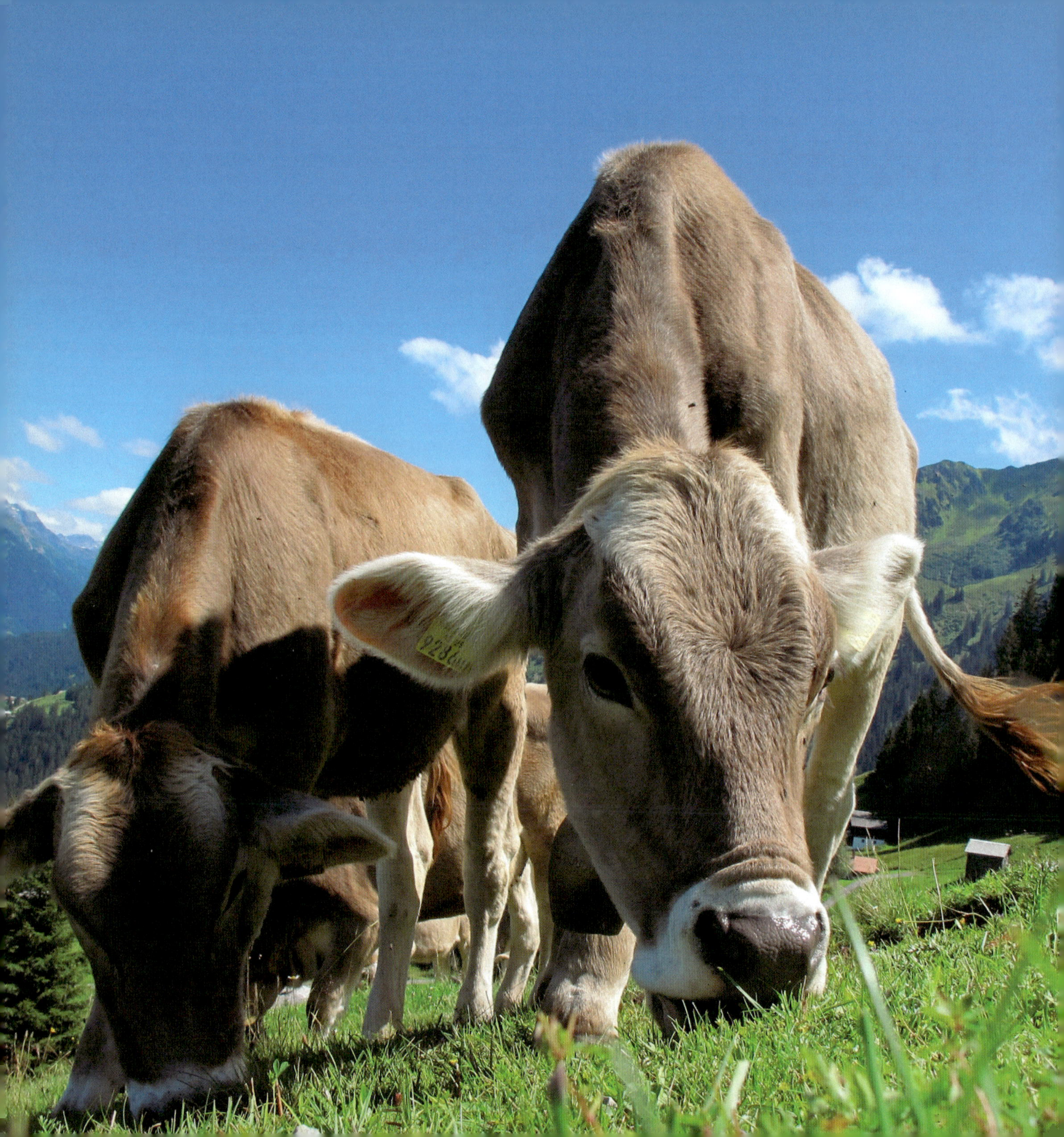

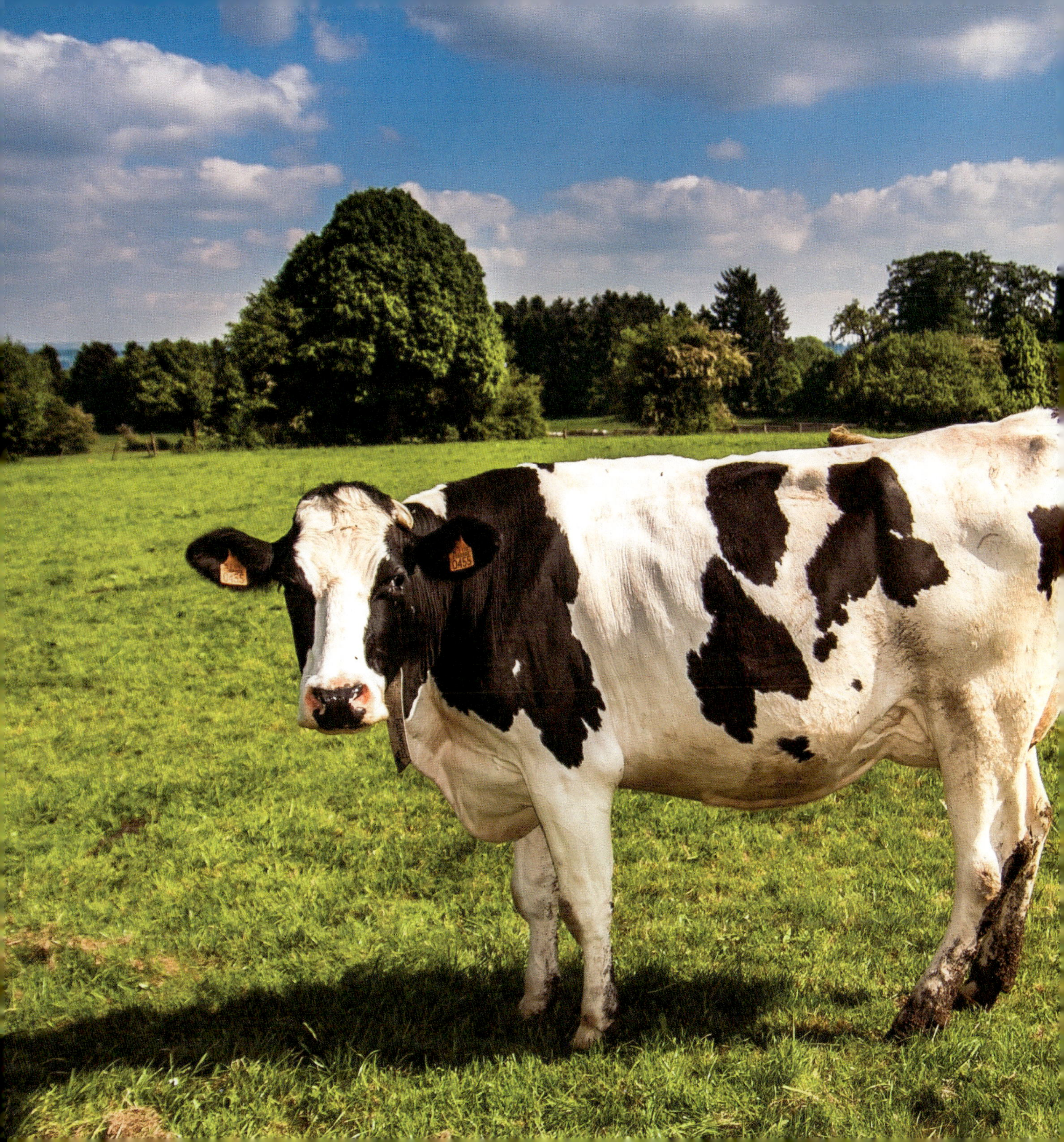
0455

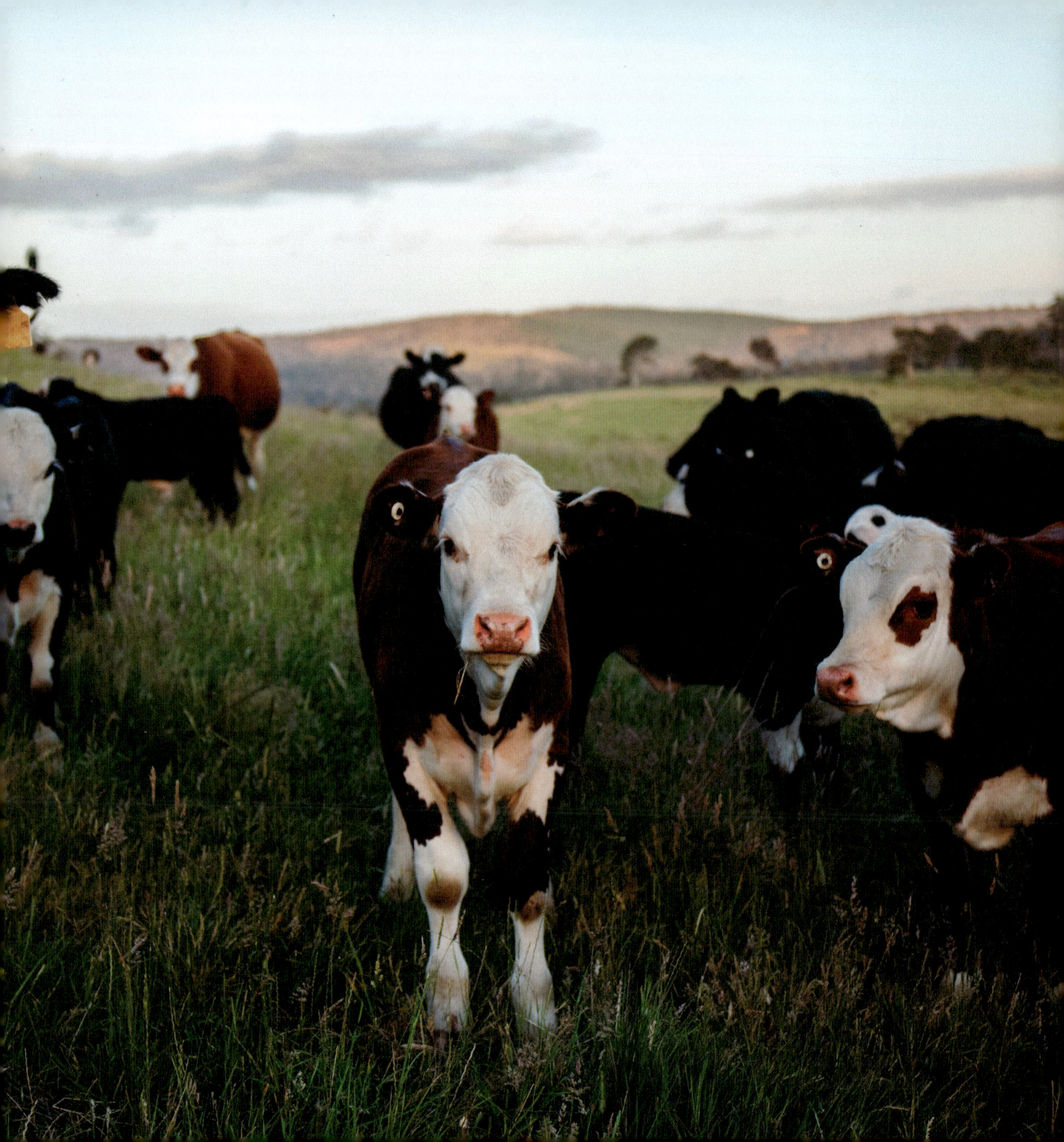

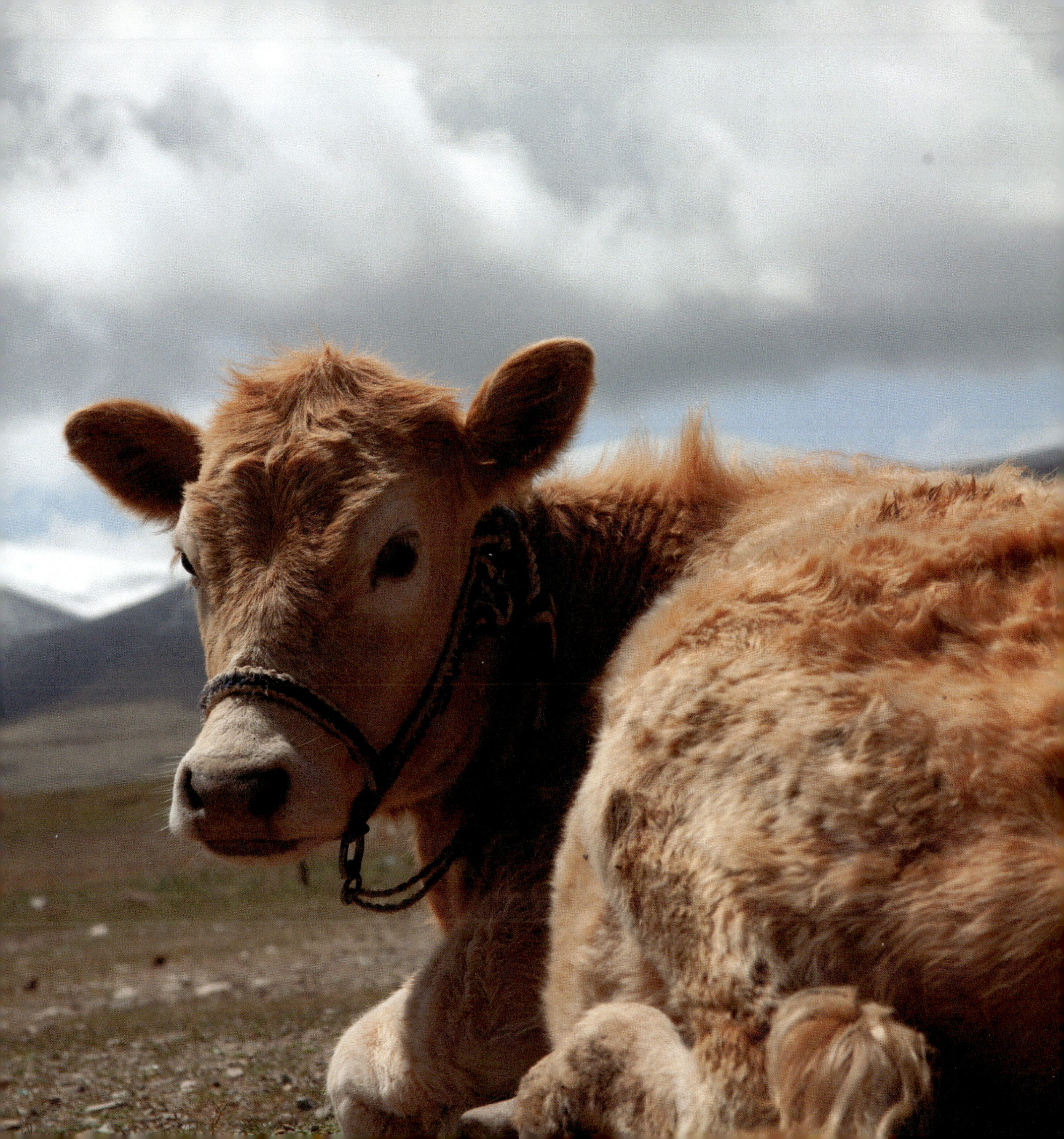

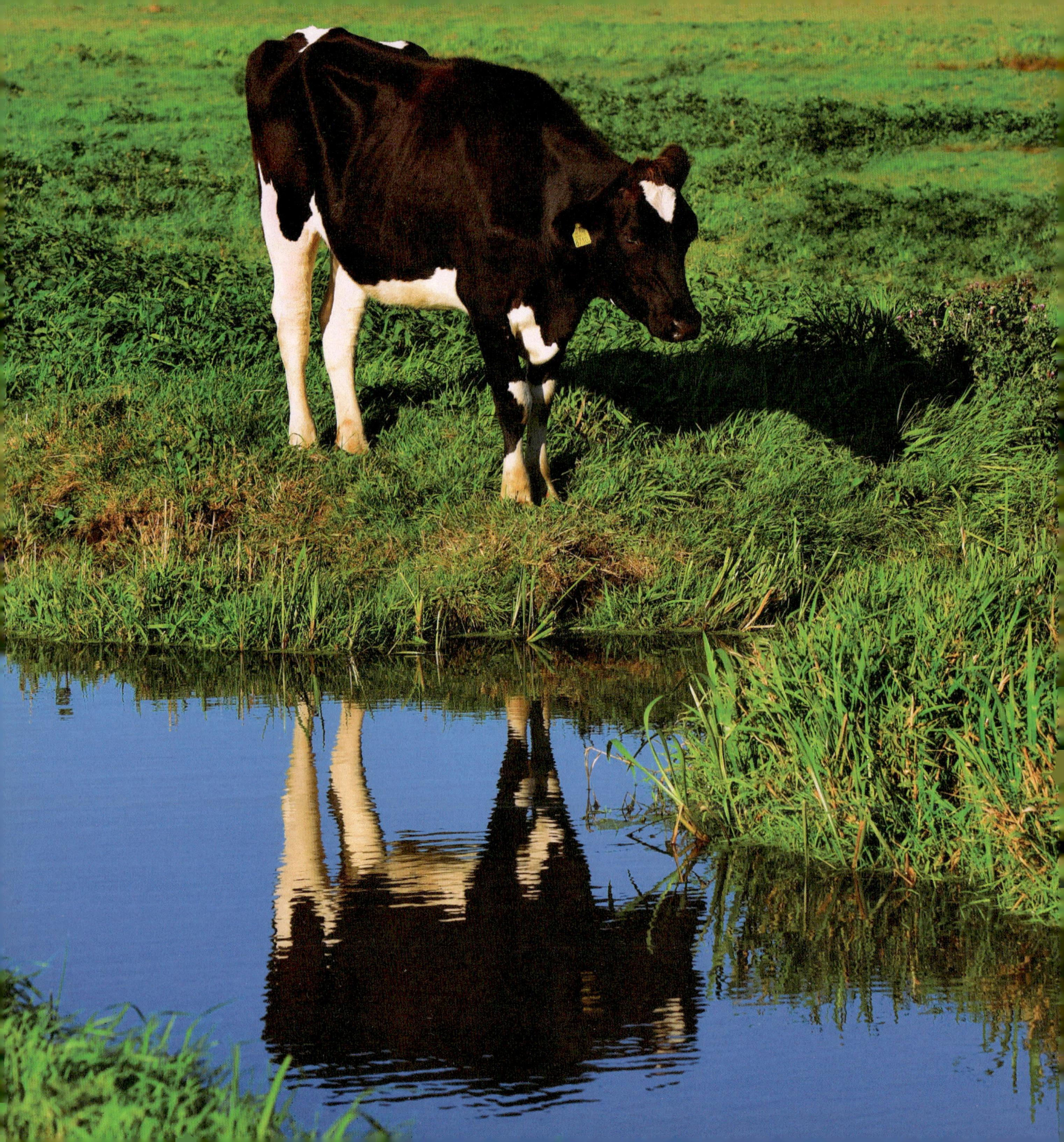

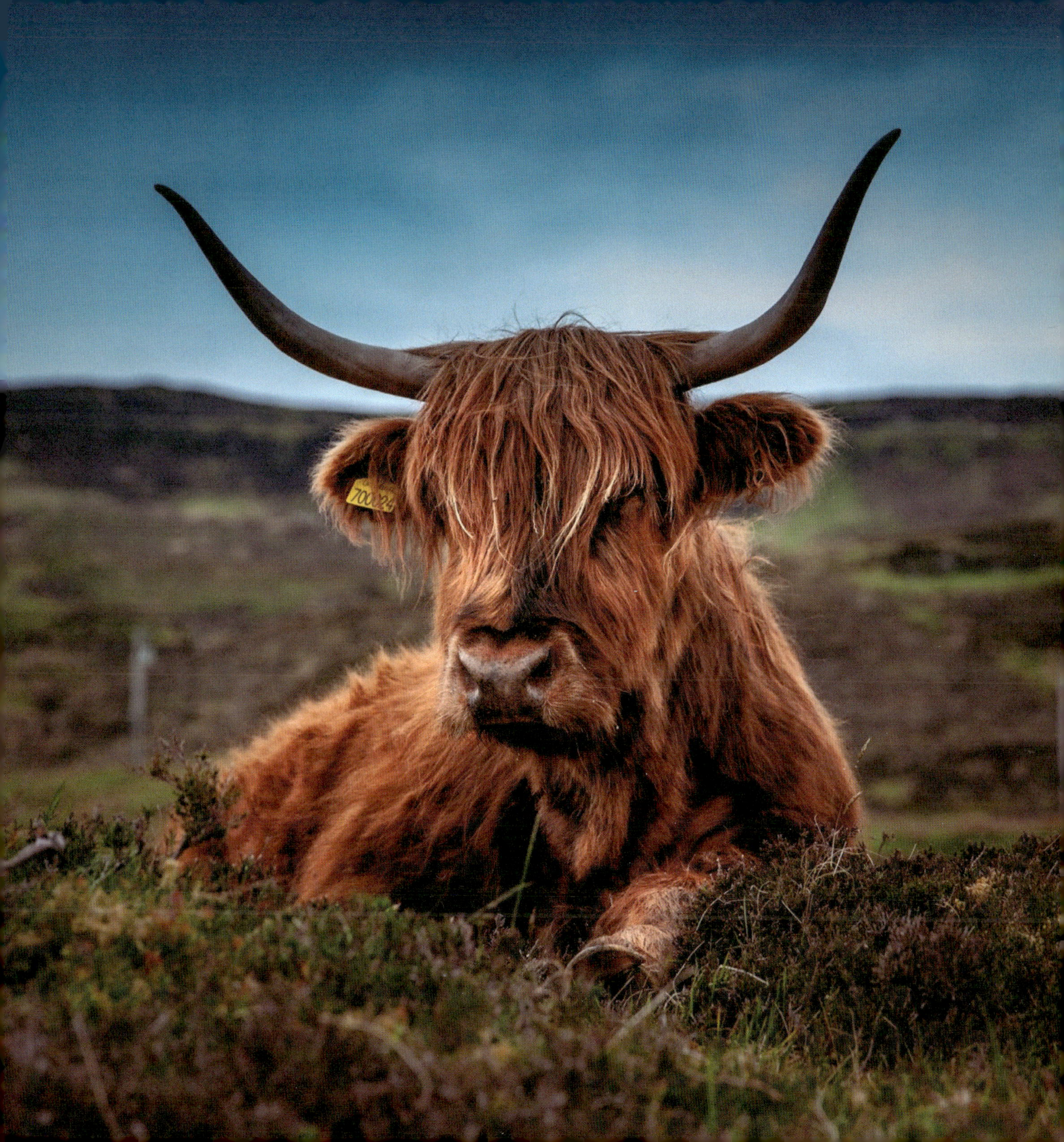

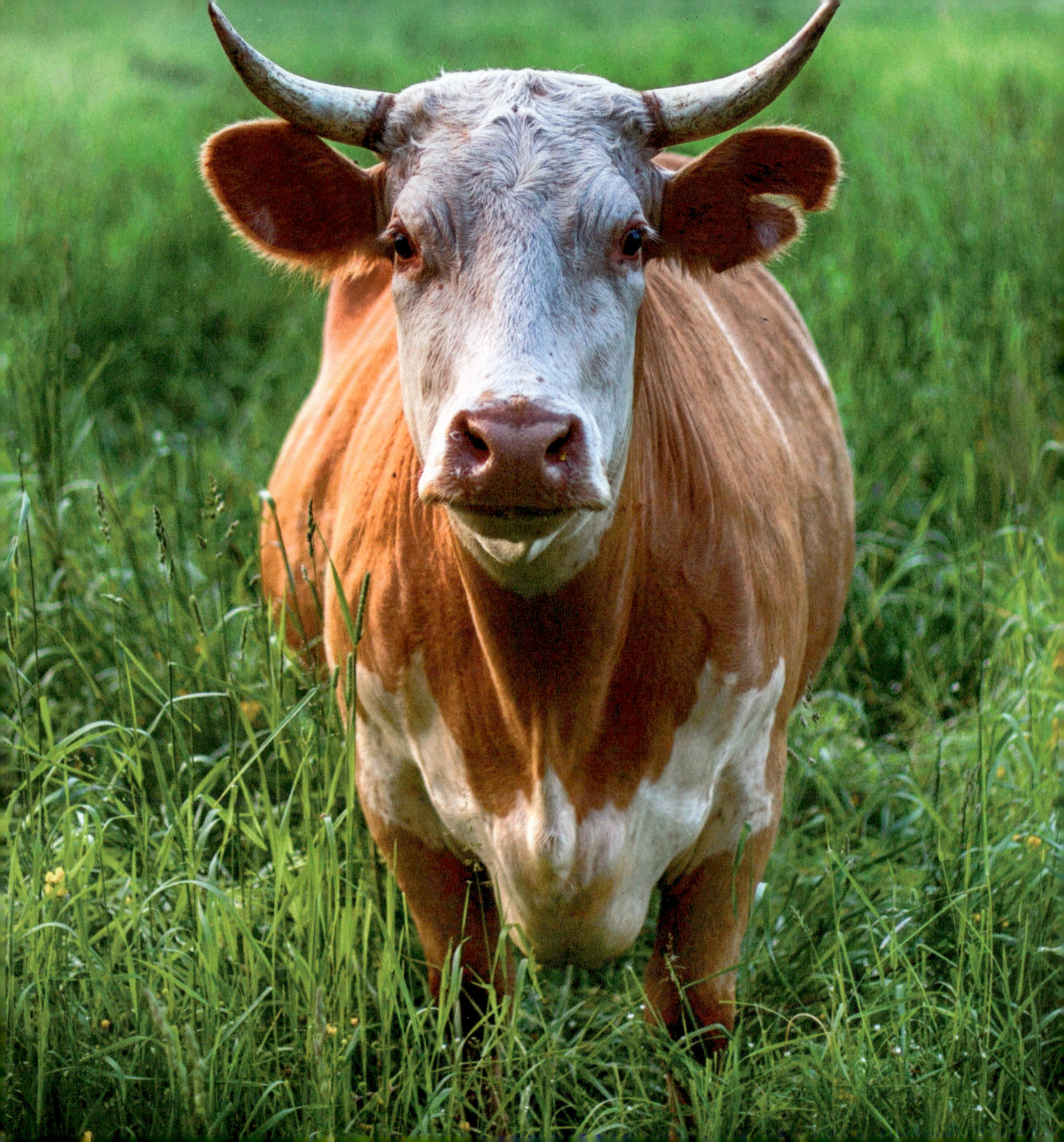

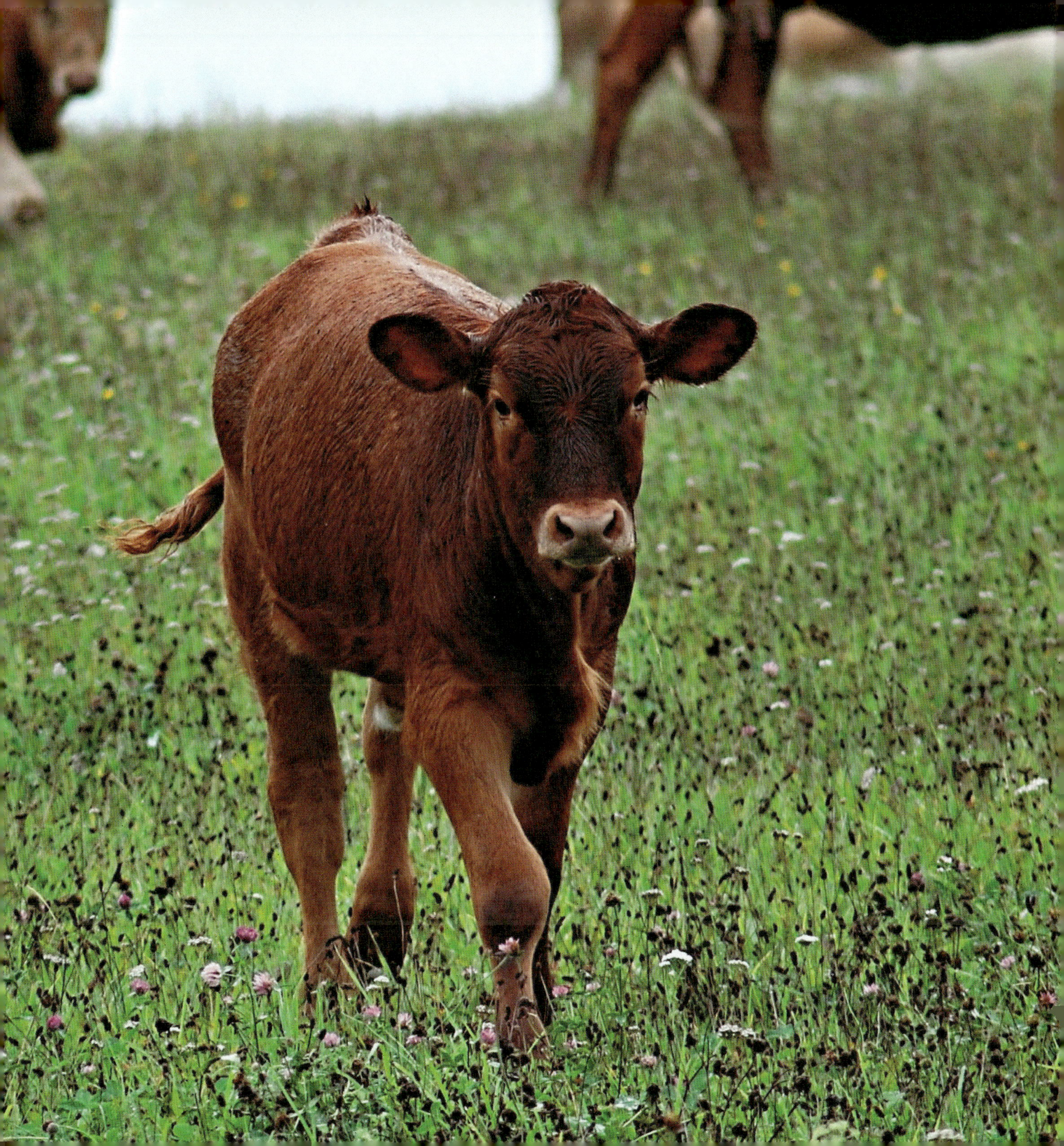

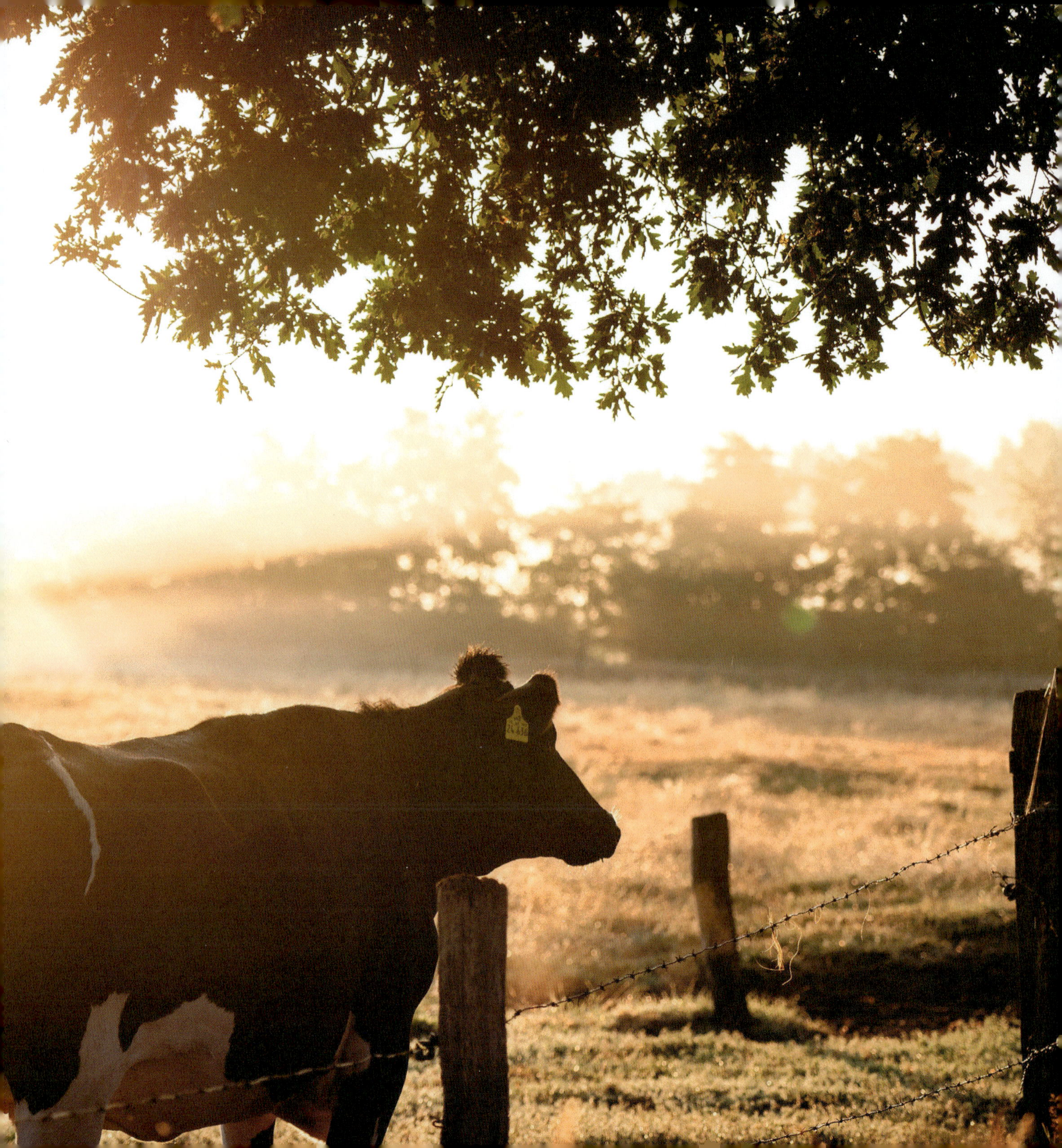

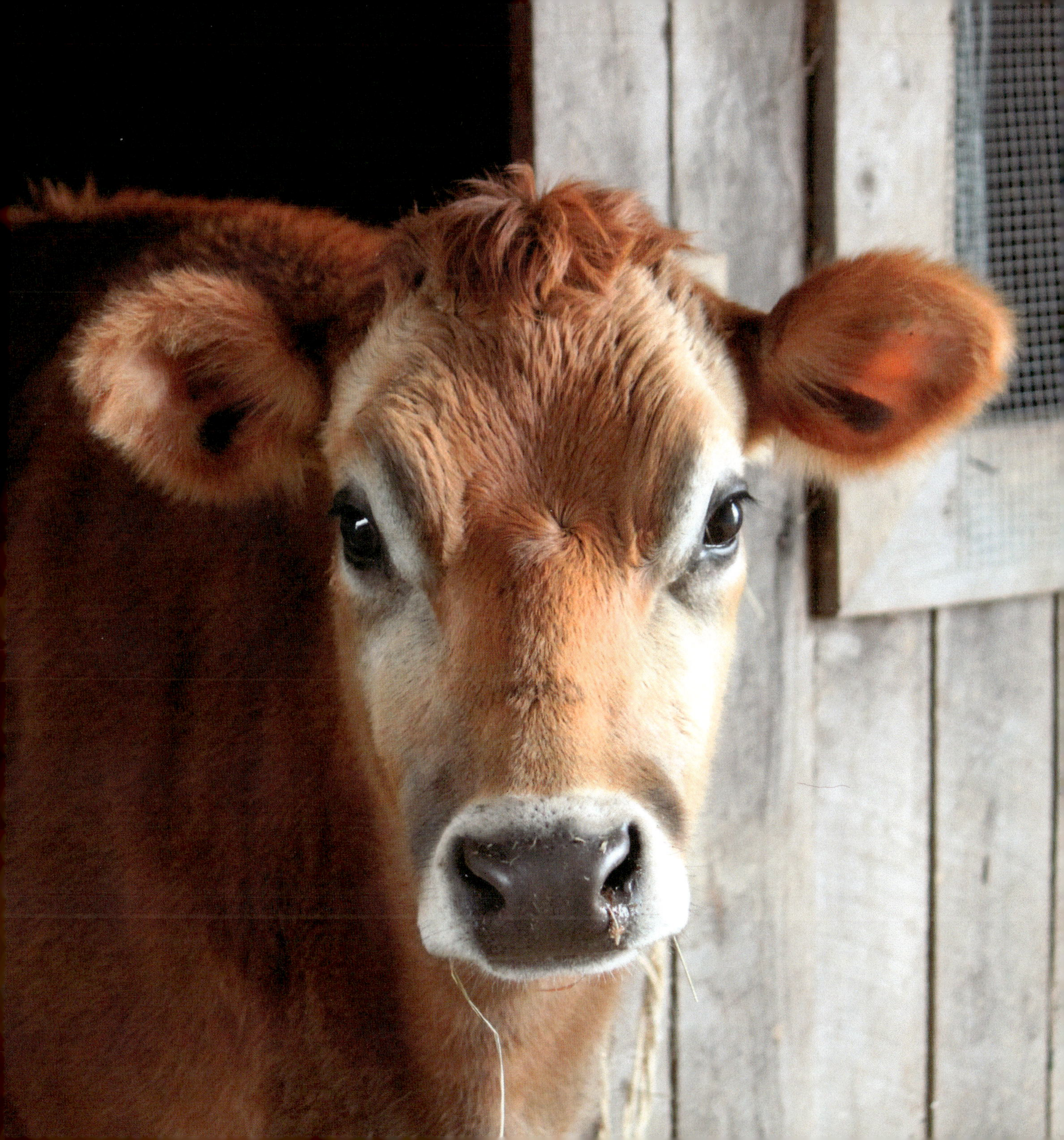

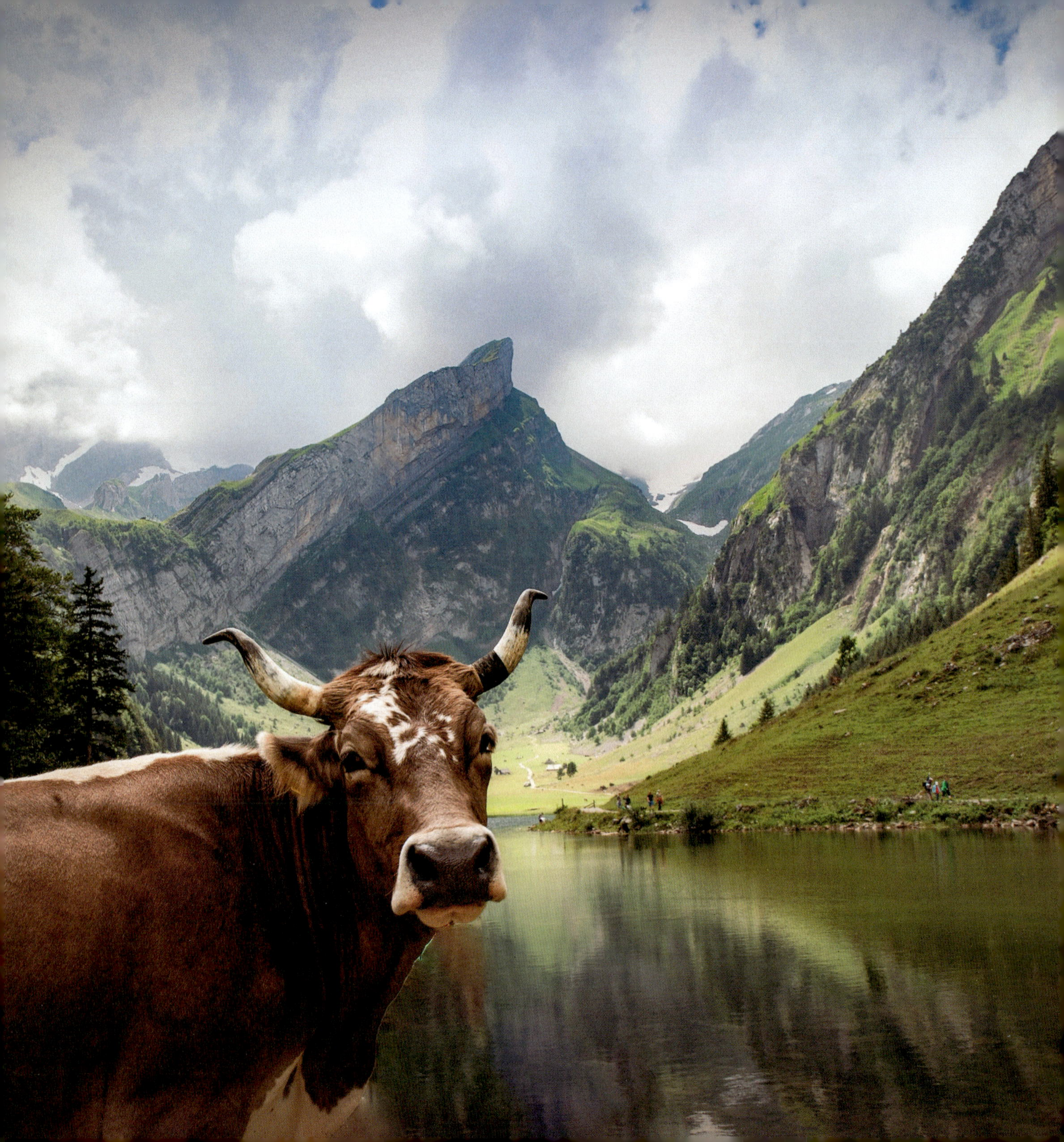

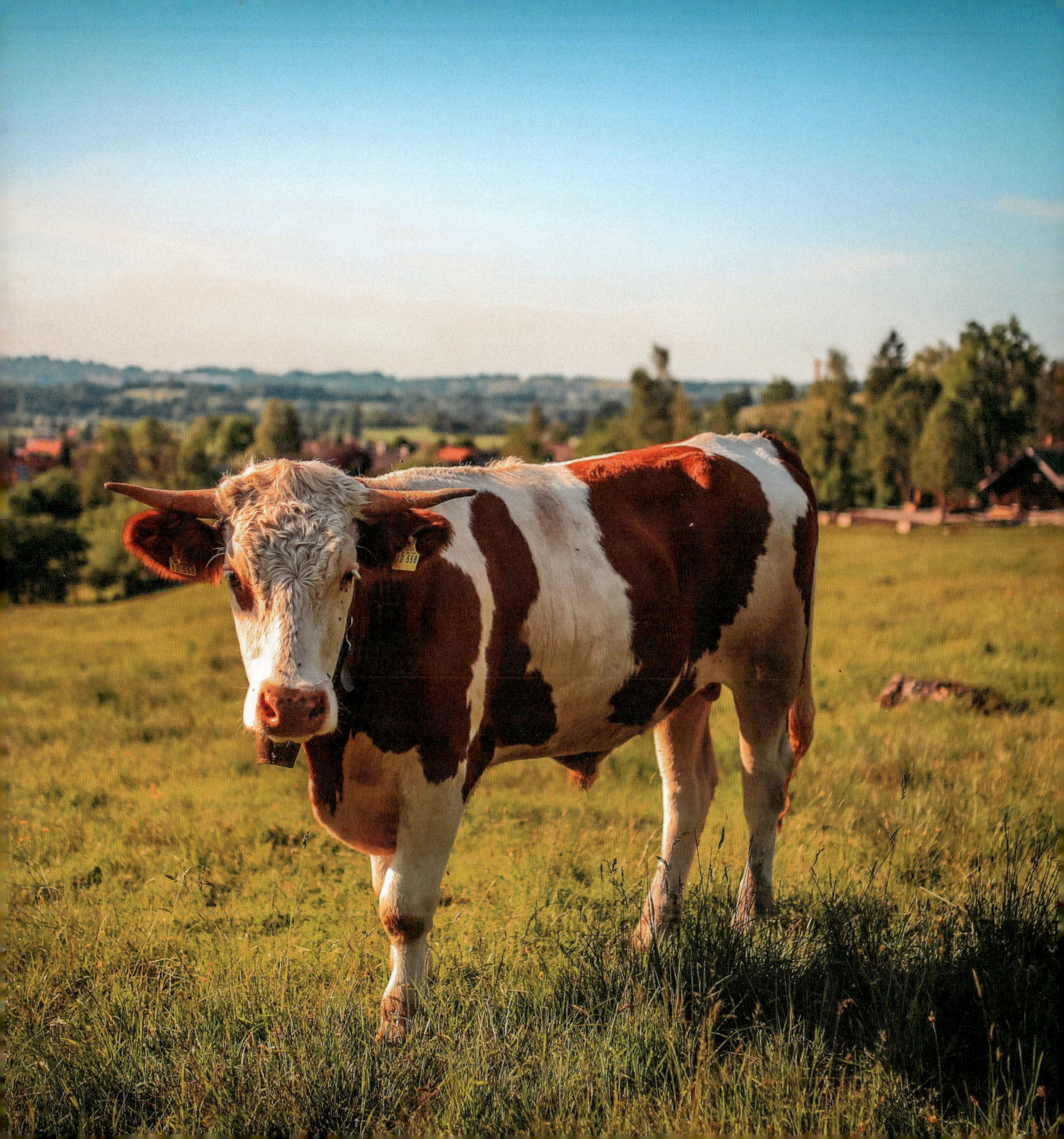

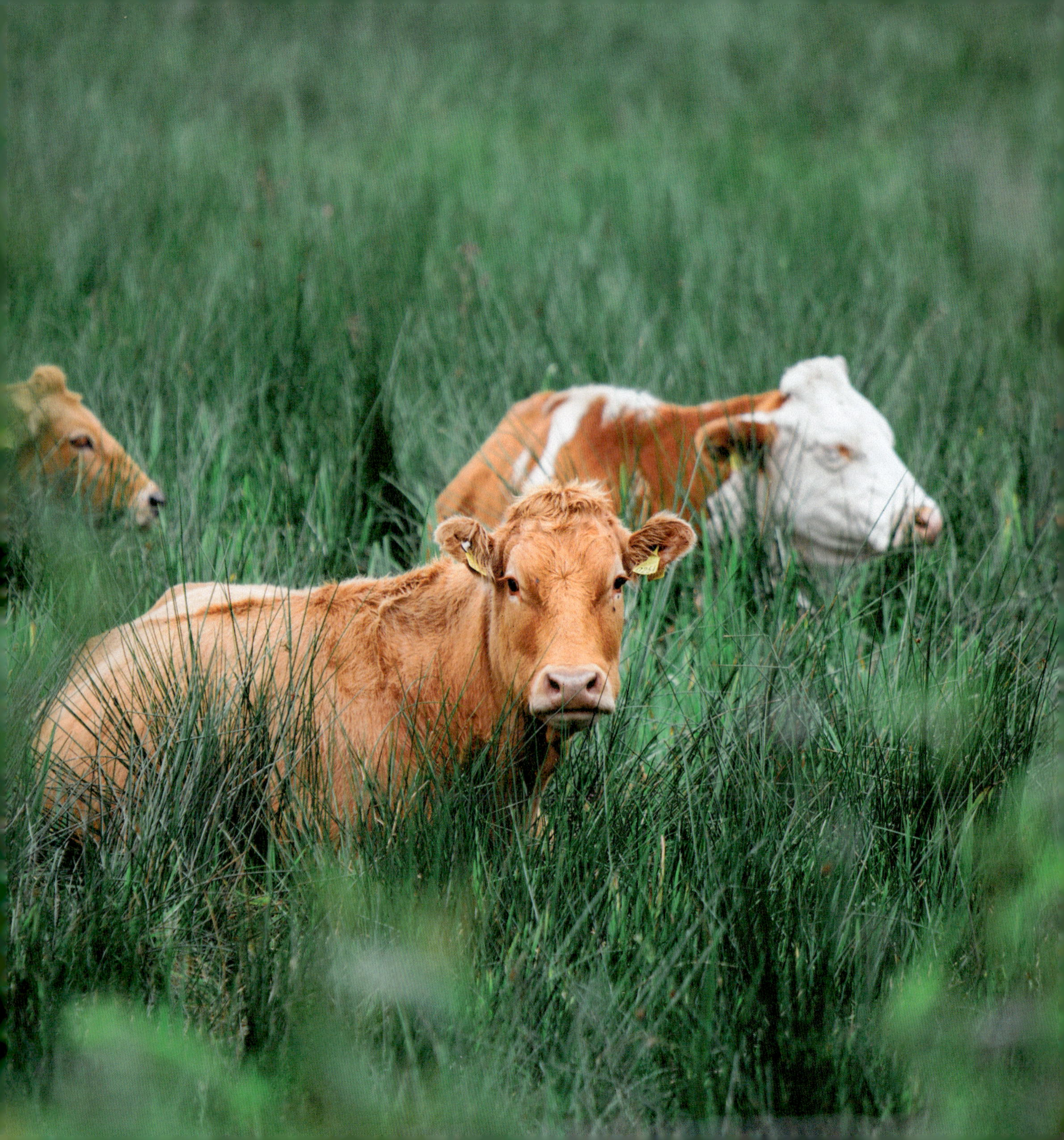

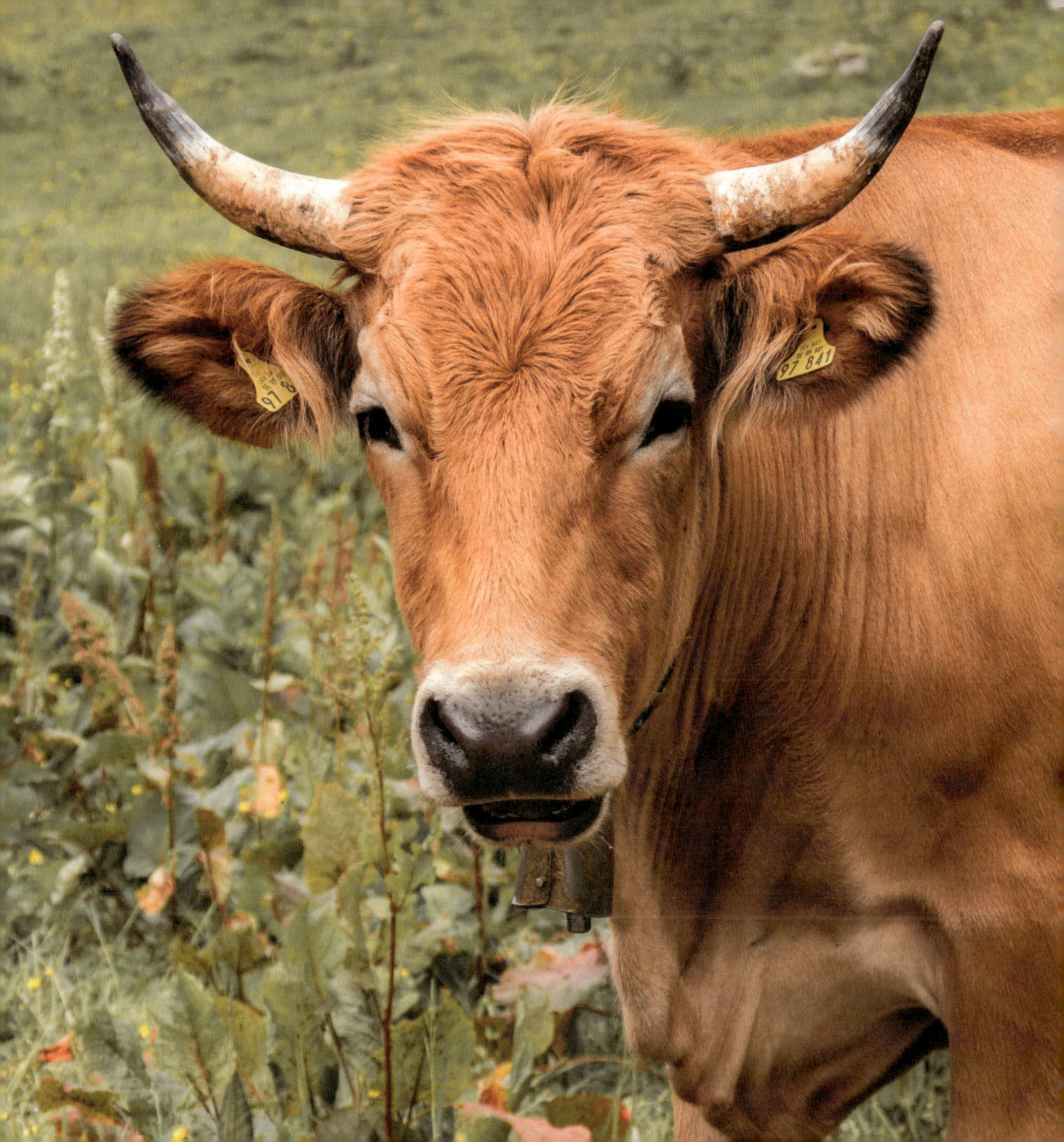
97 841

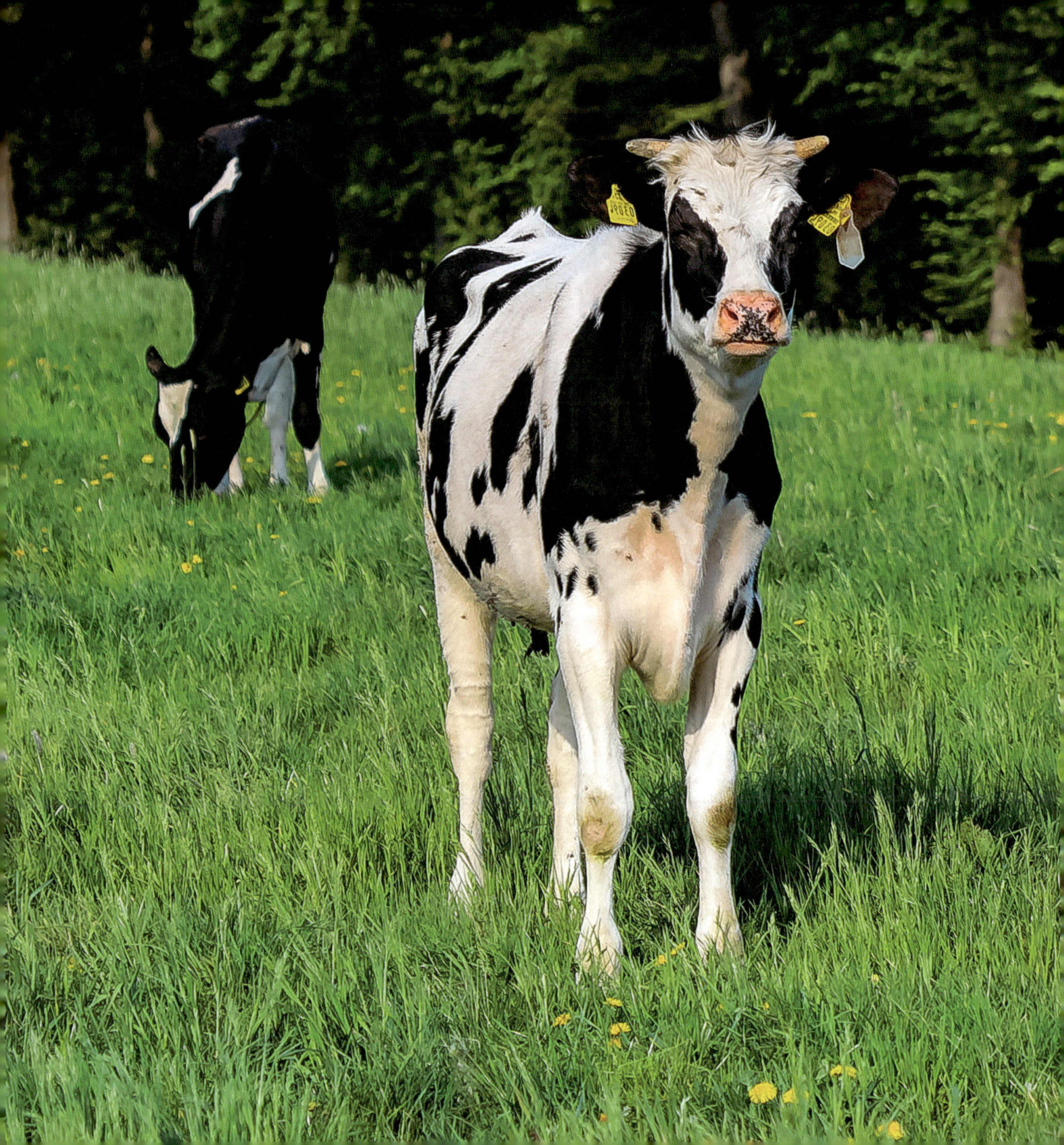

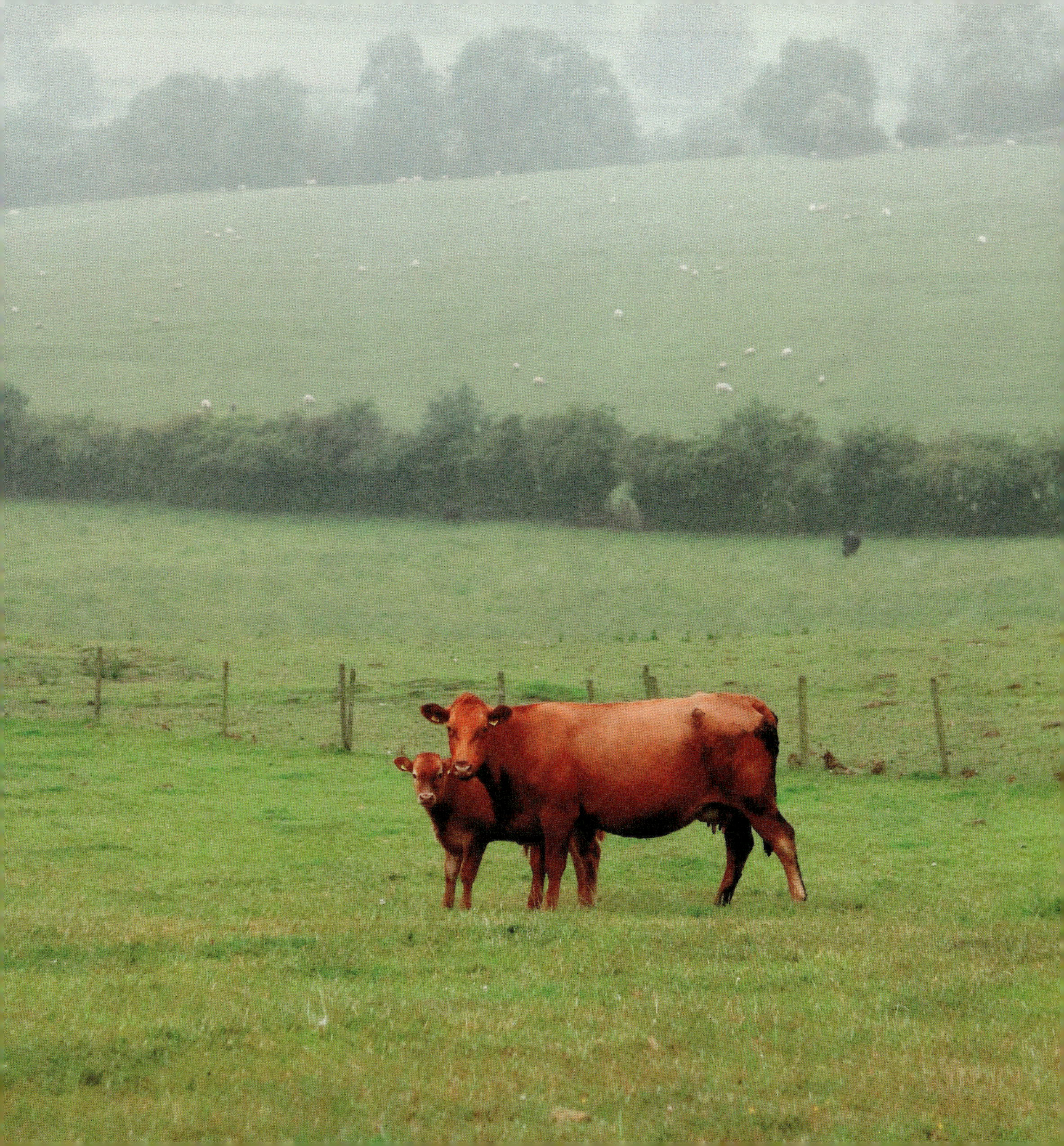

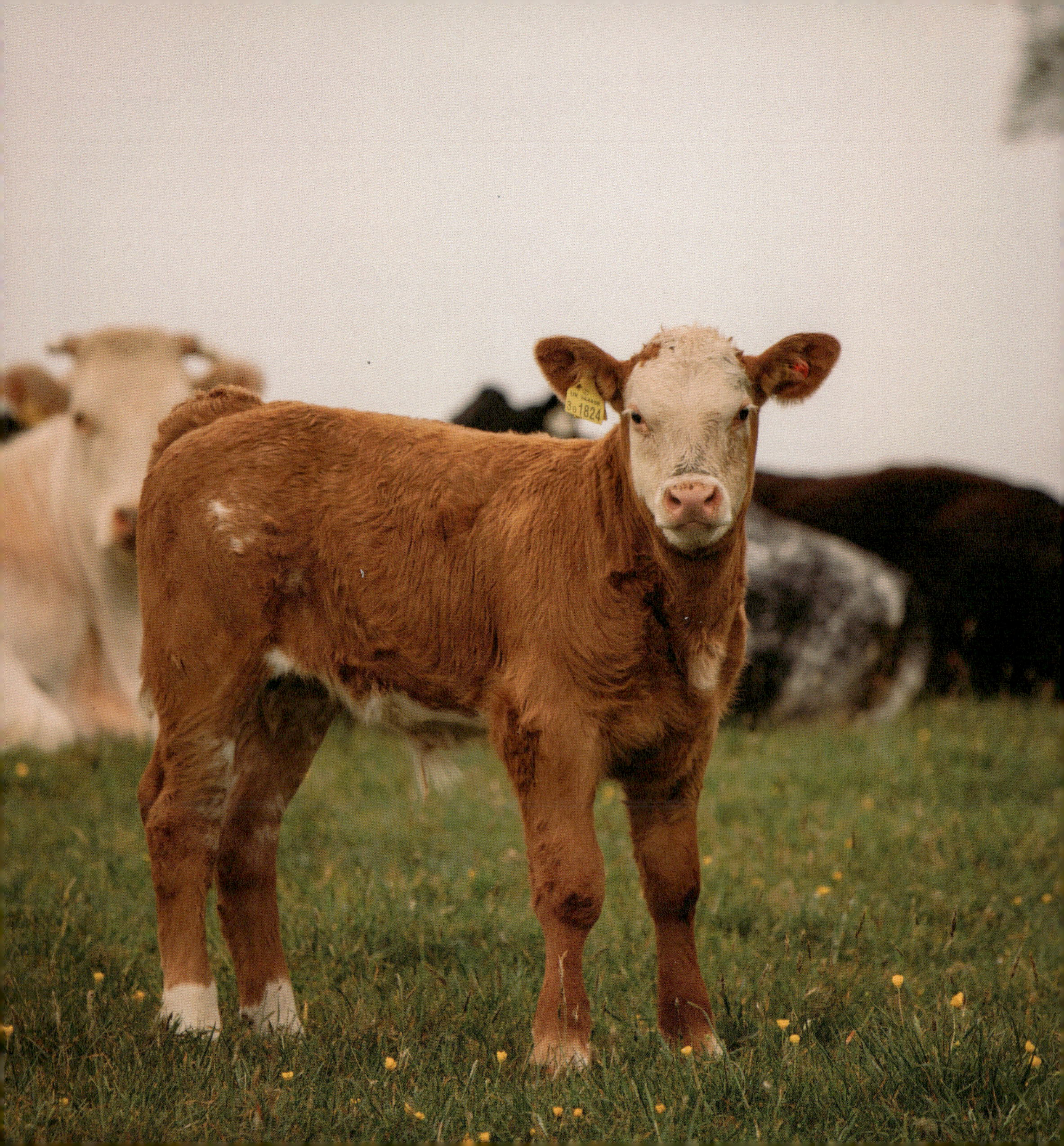
30 1824

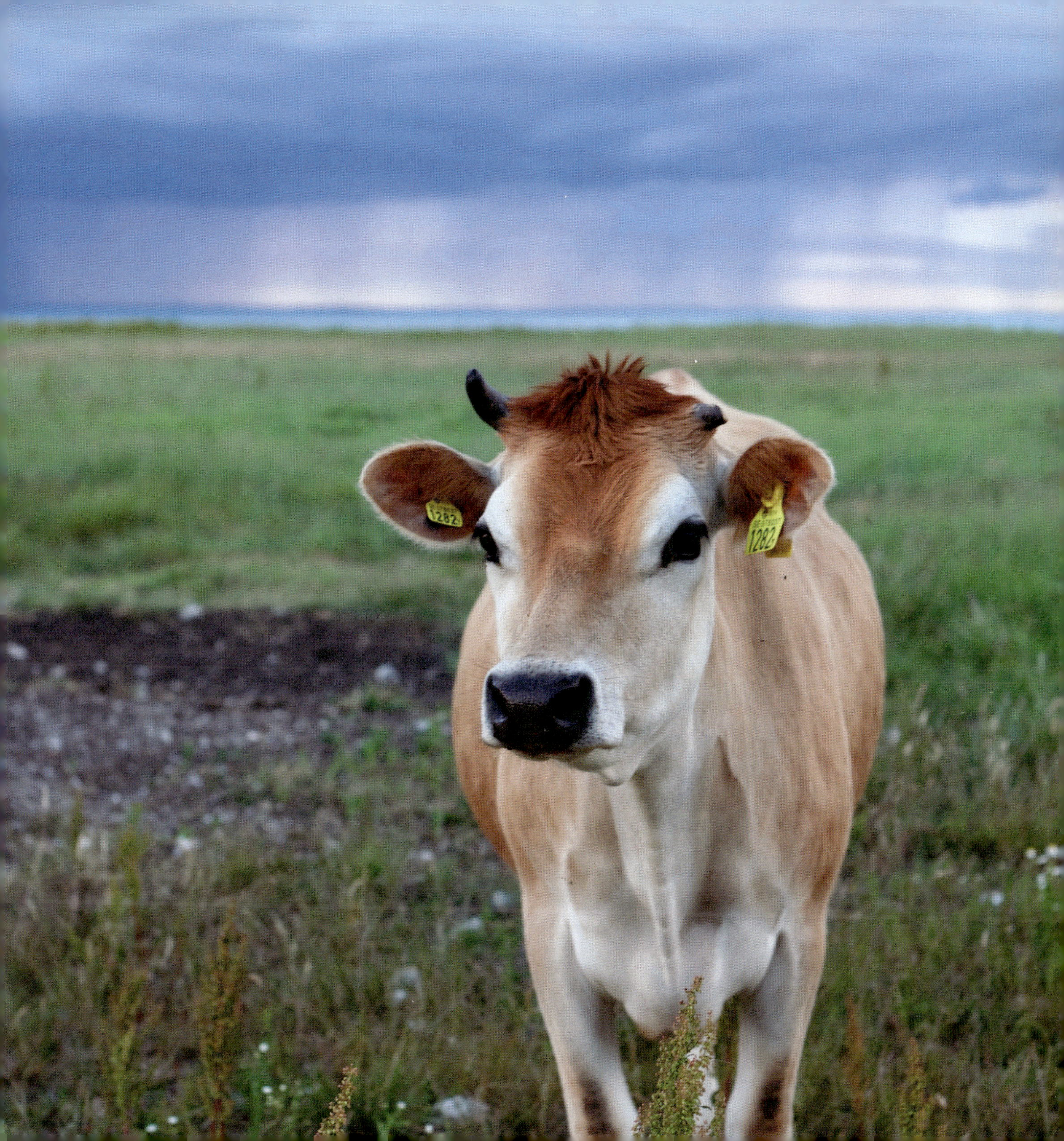
1282
1282

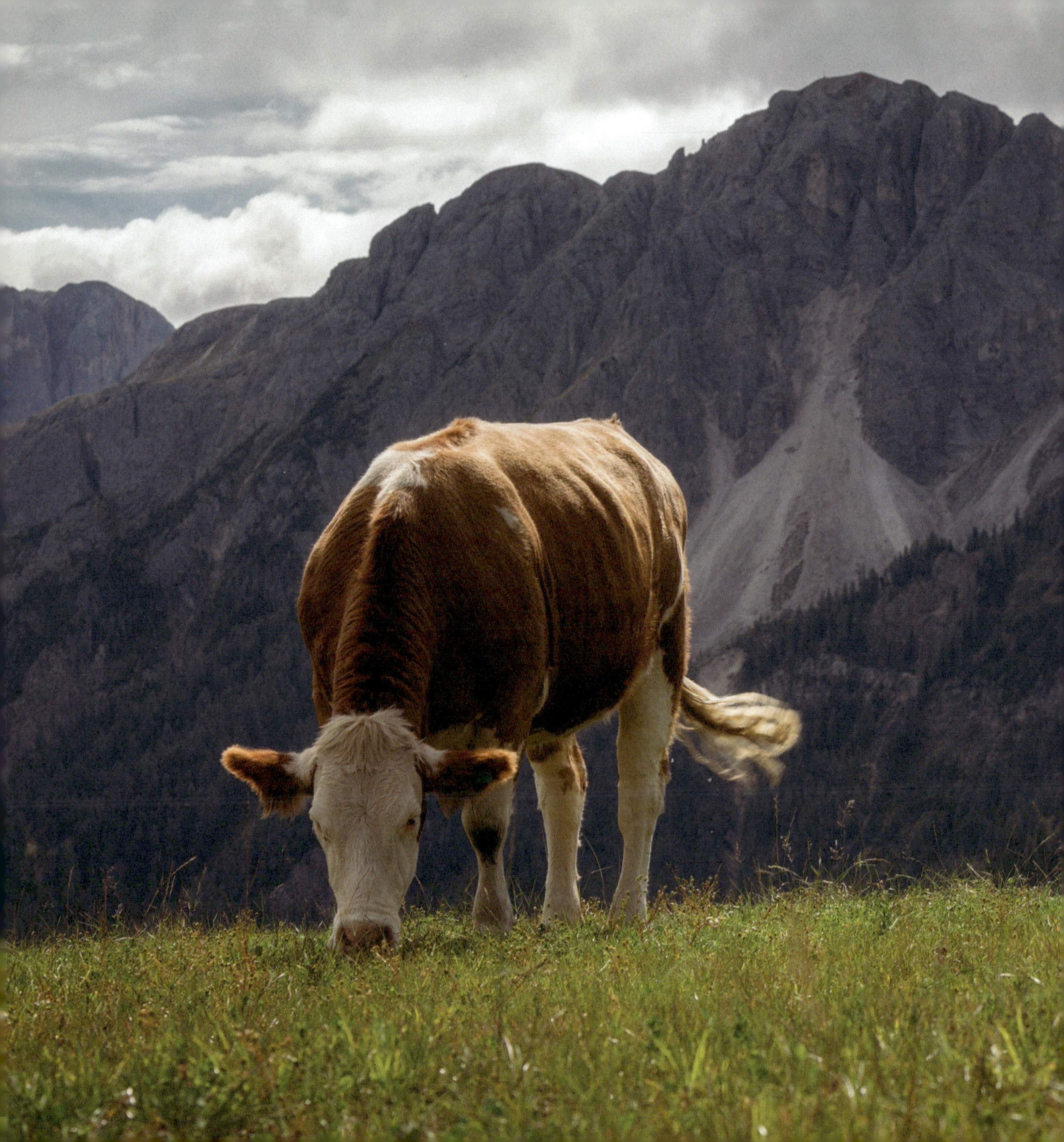

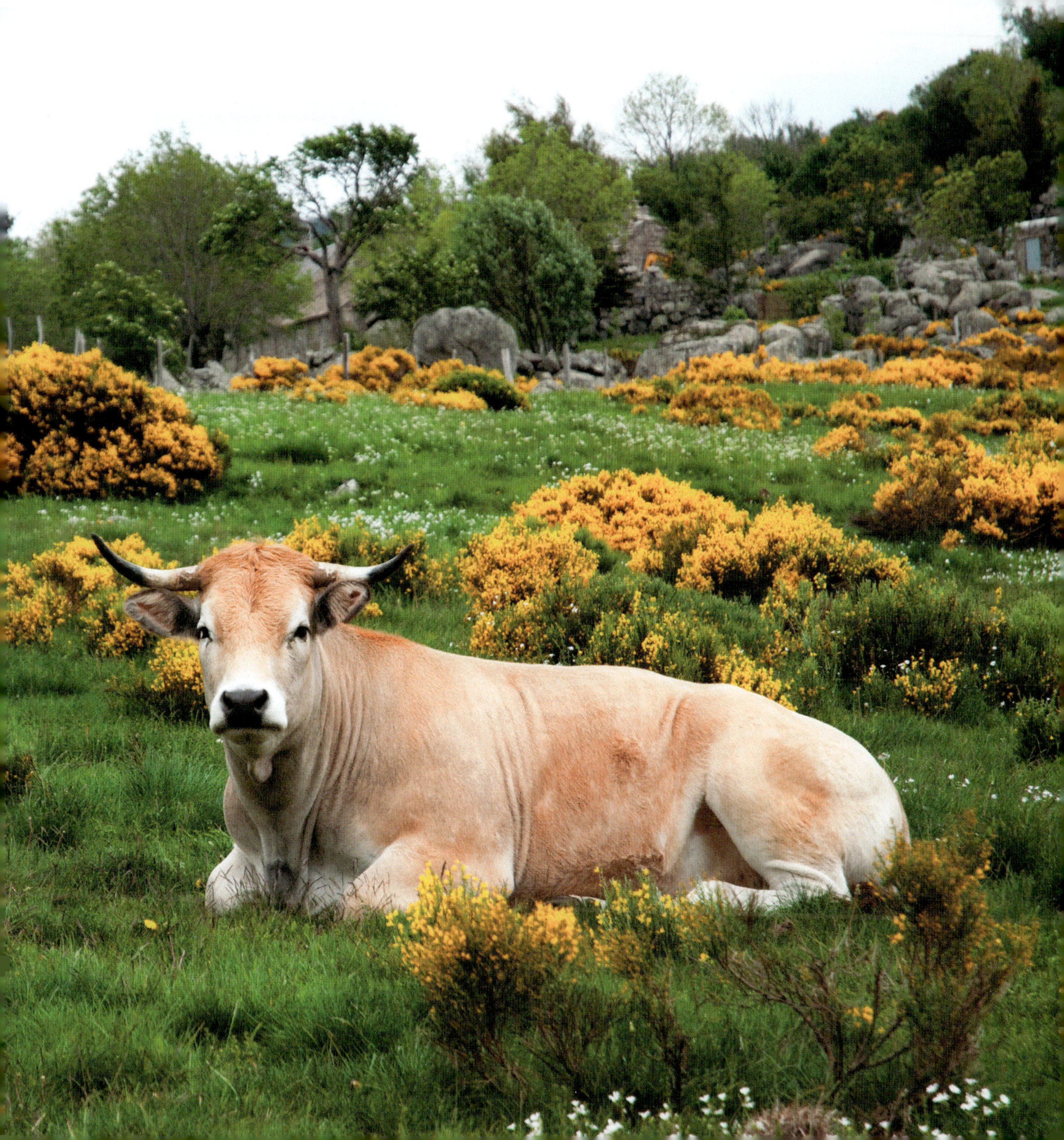

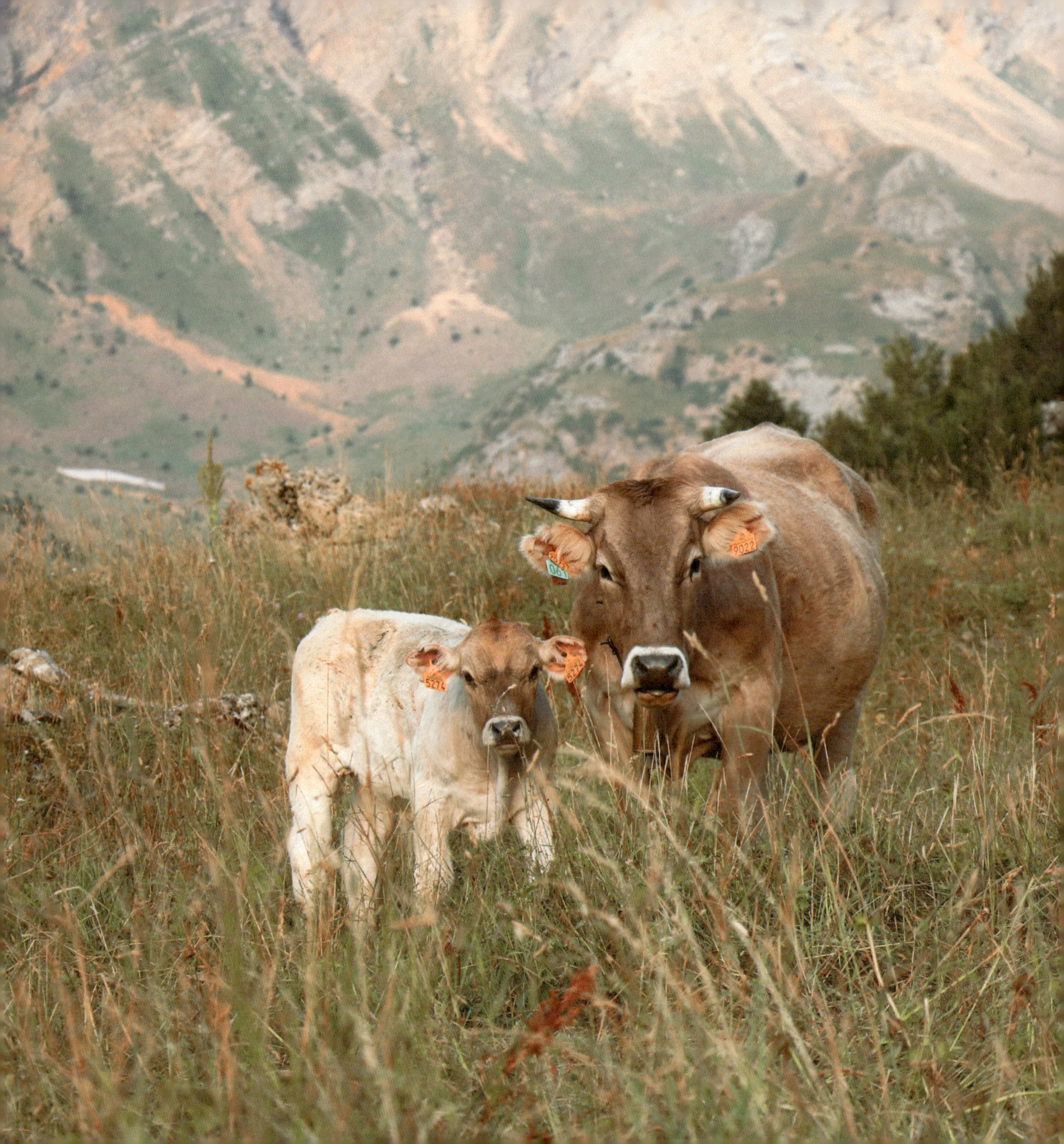

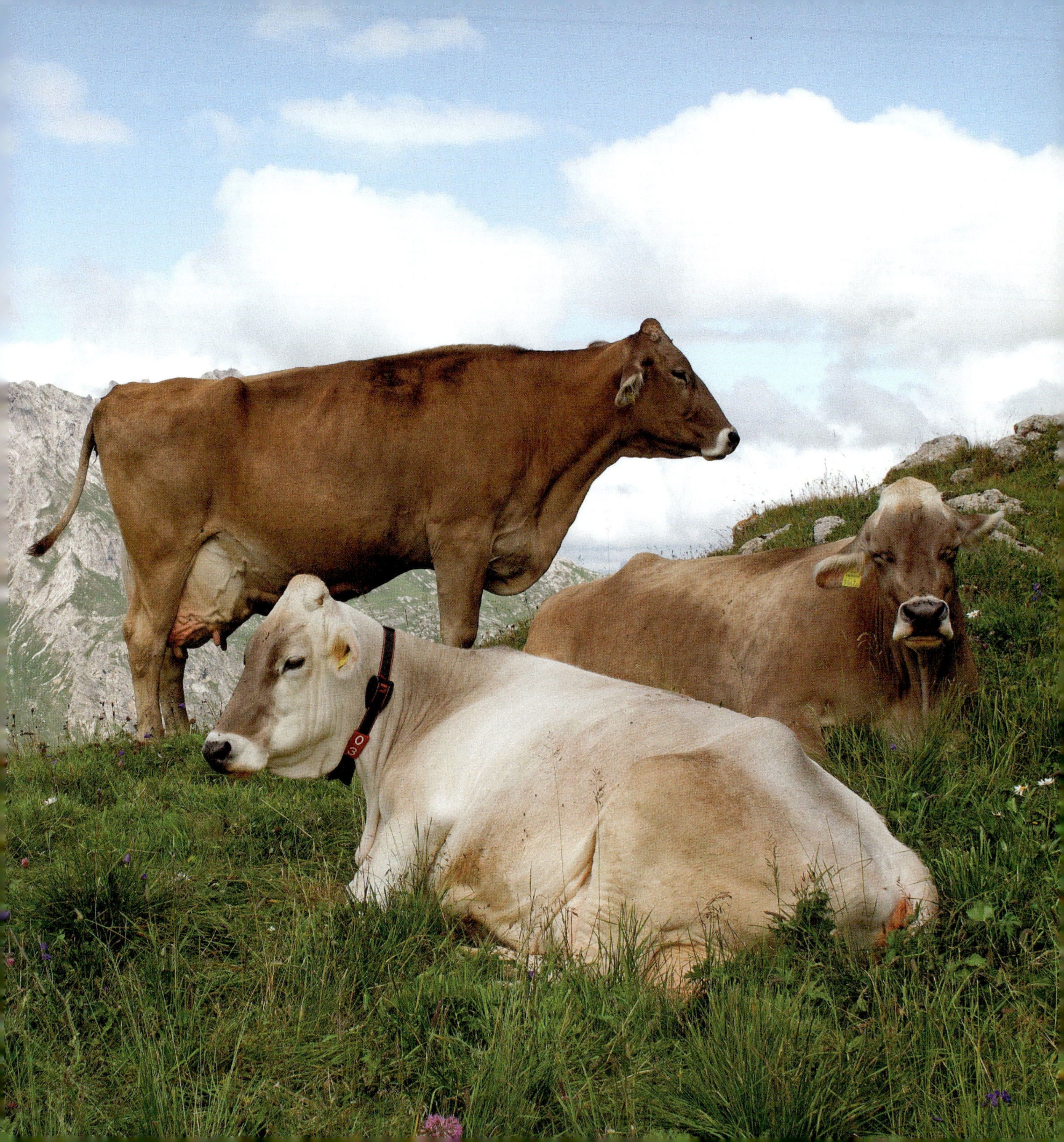
03

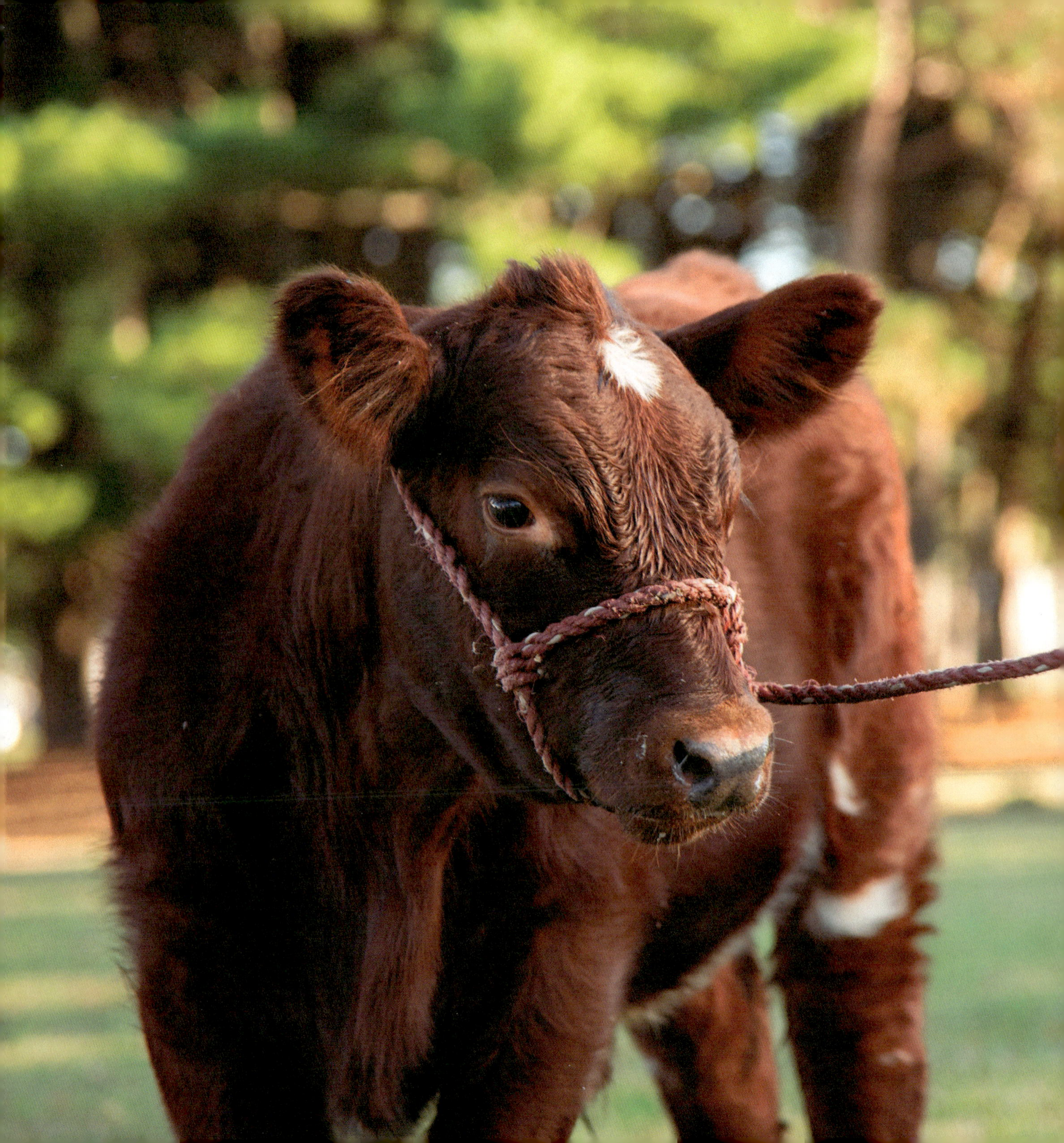

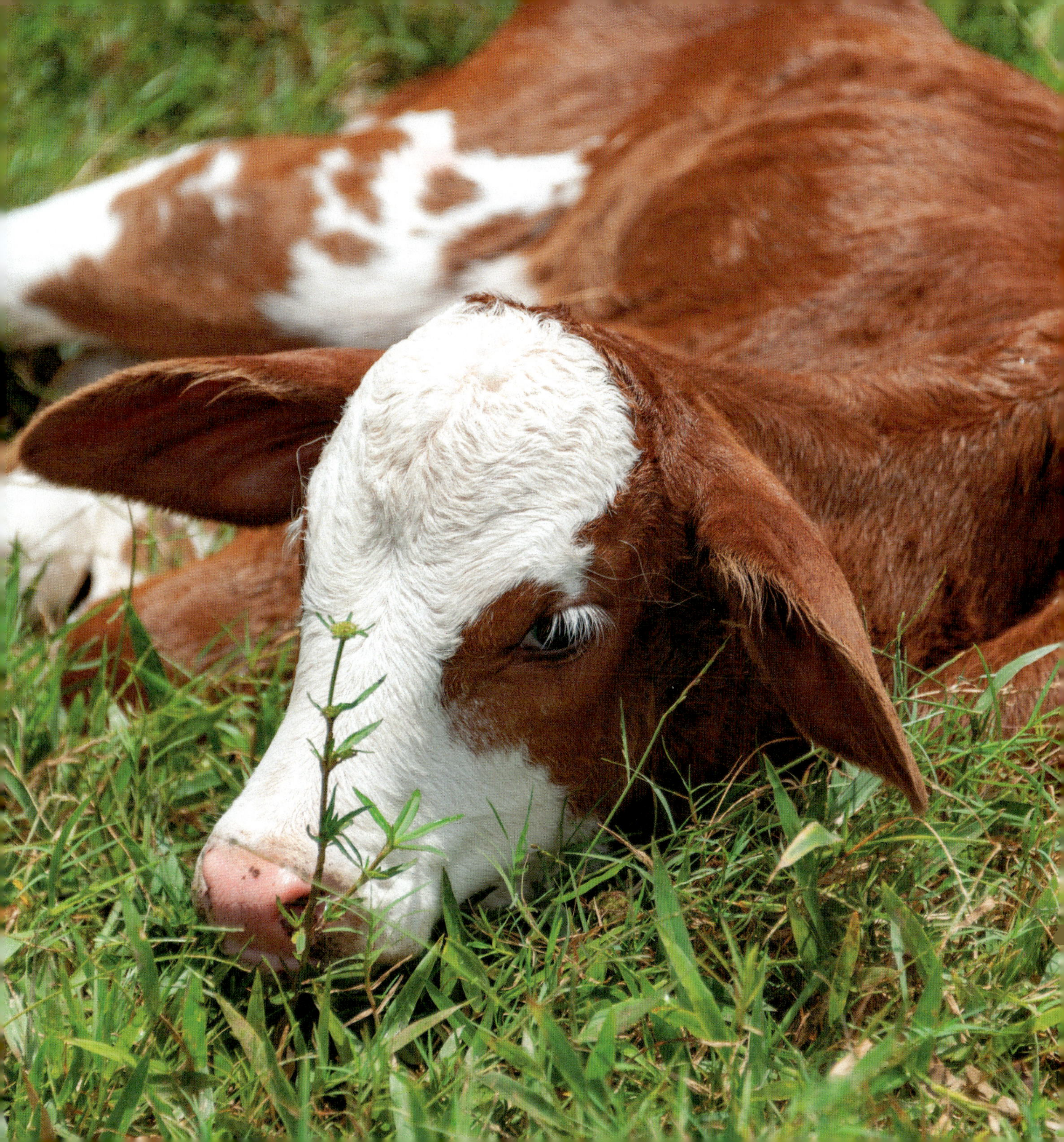

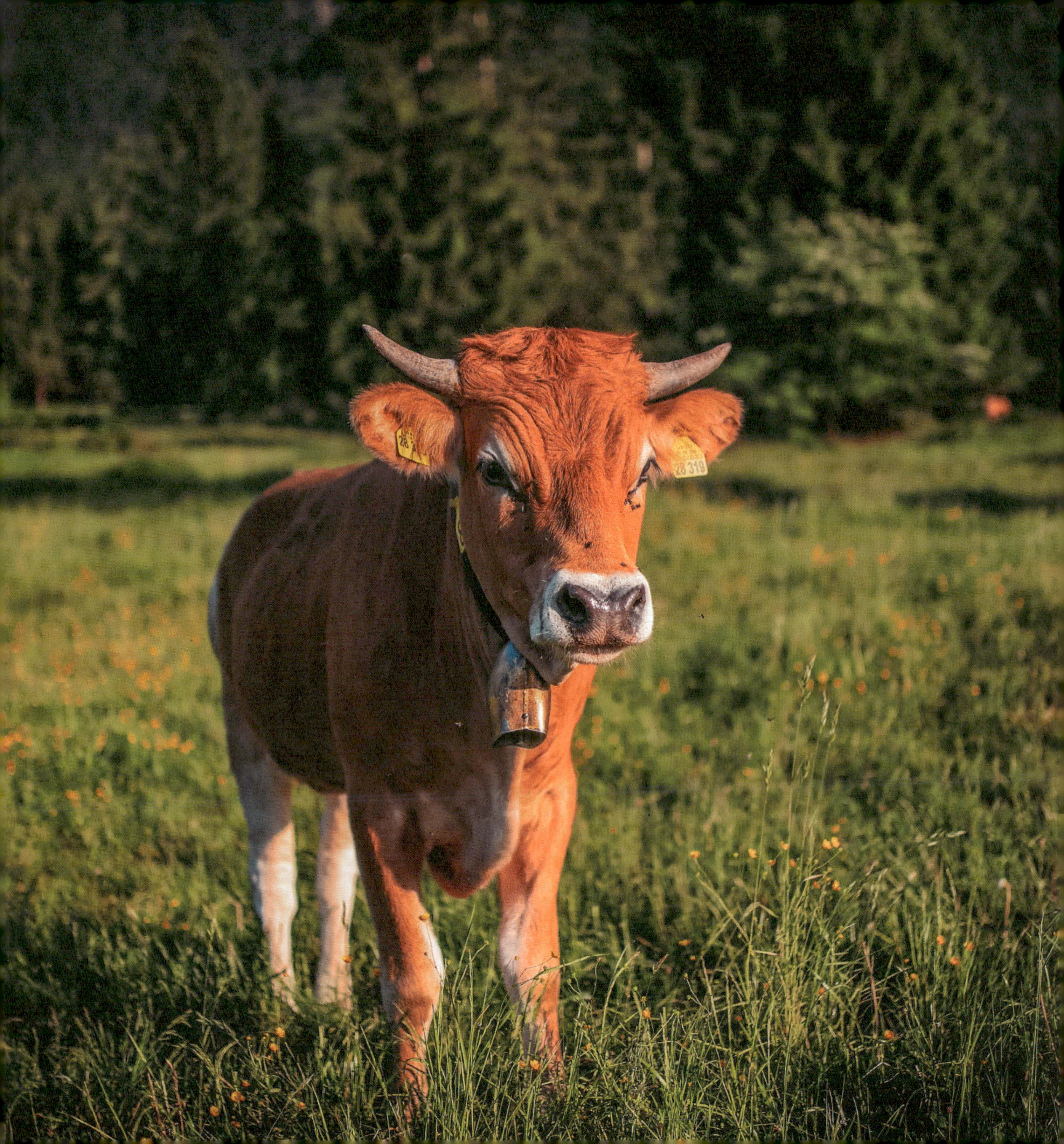
28 319

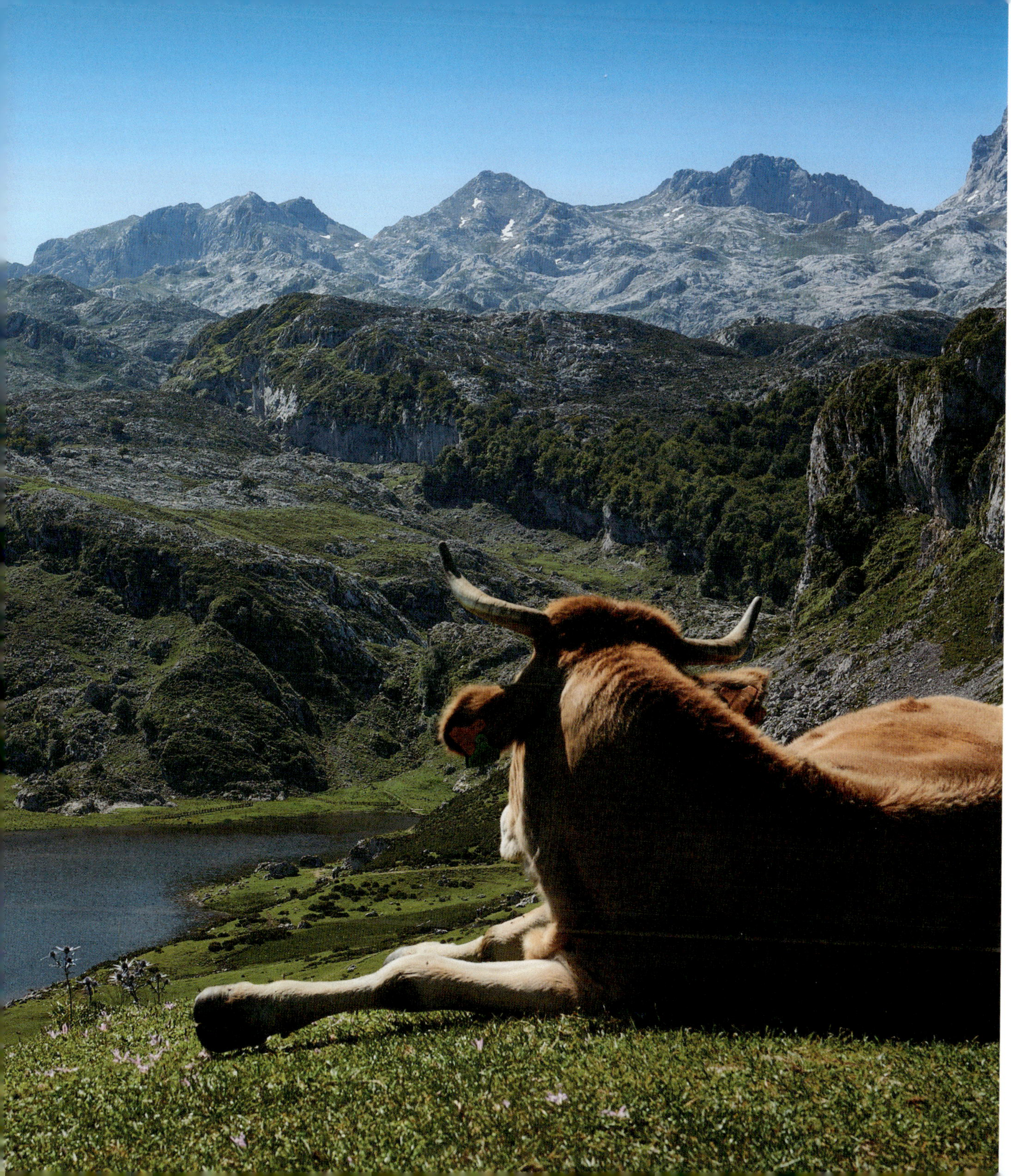

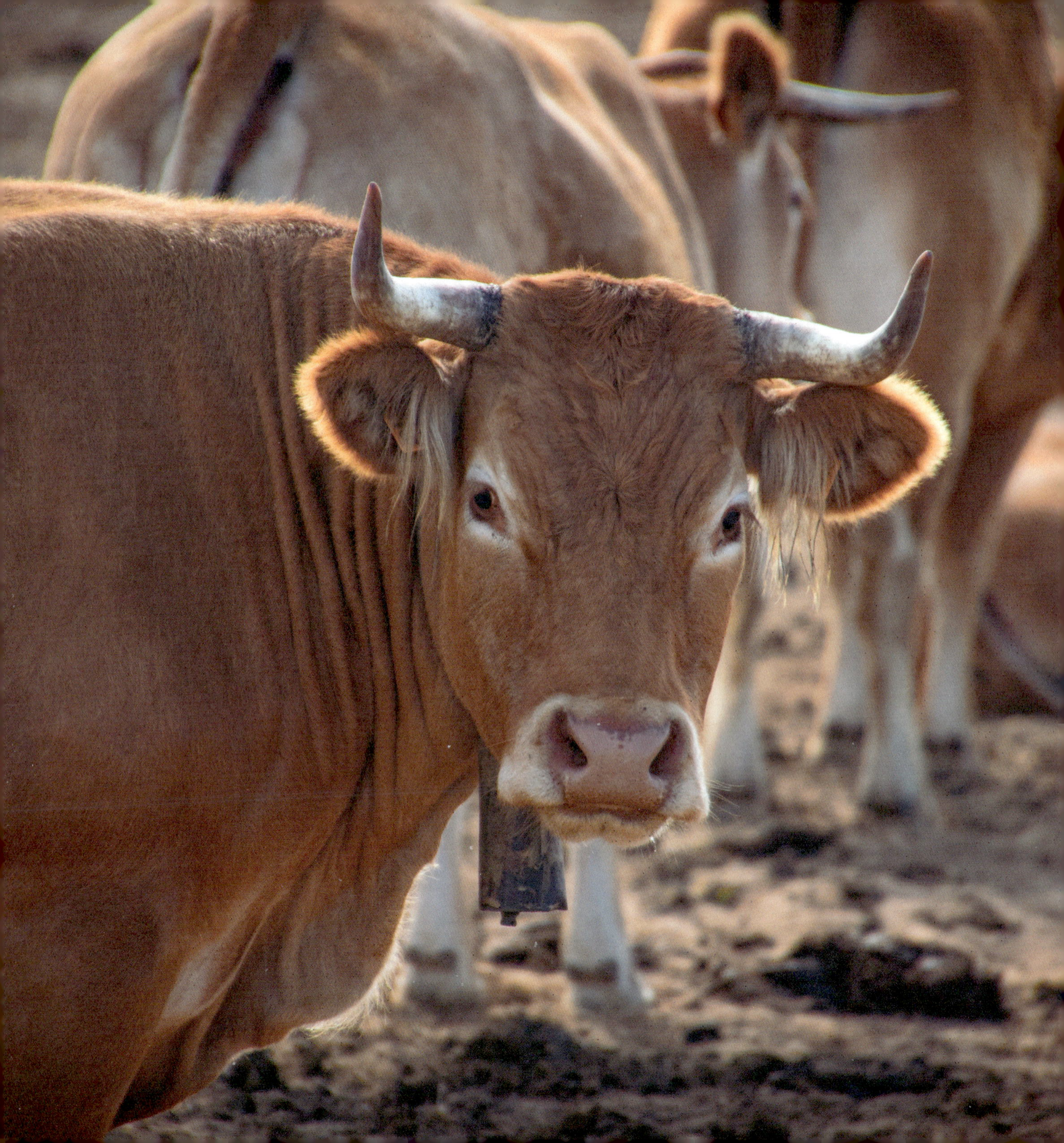

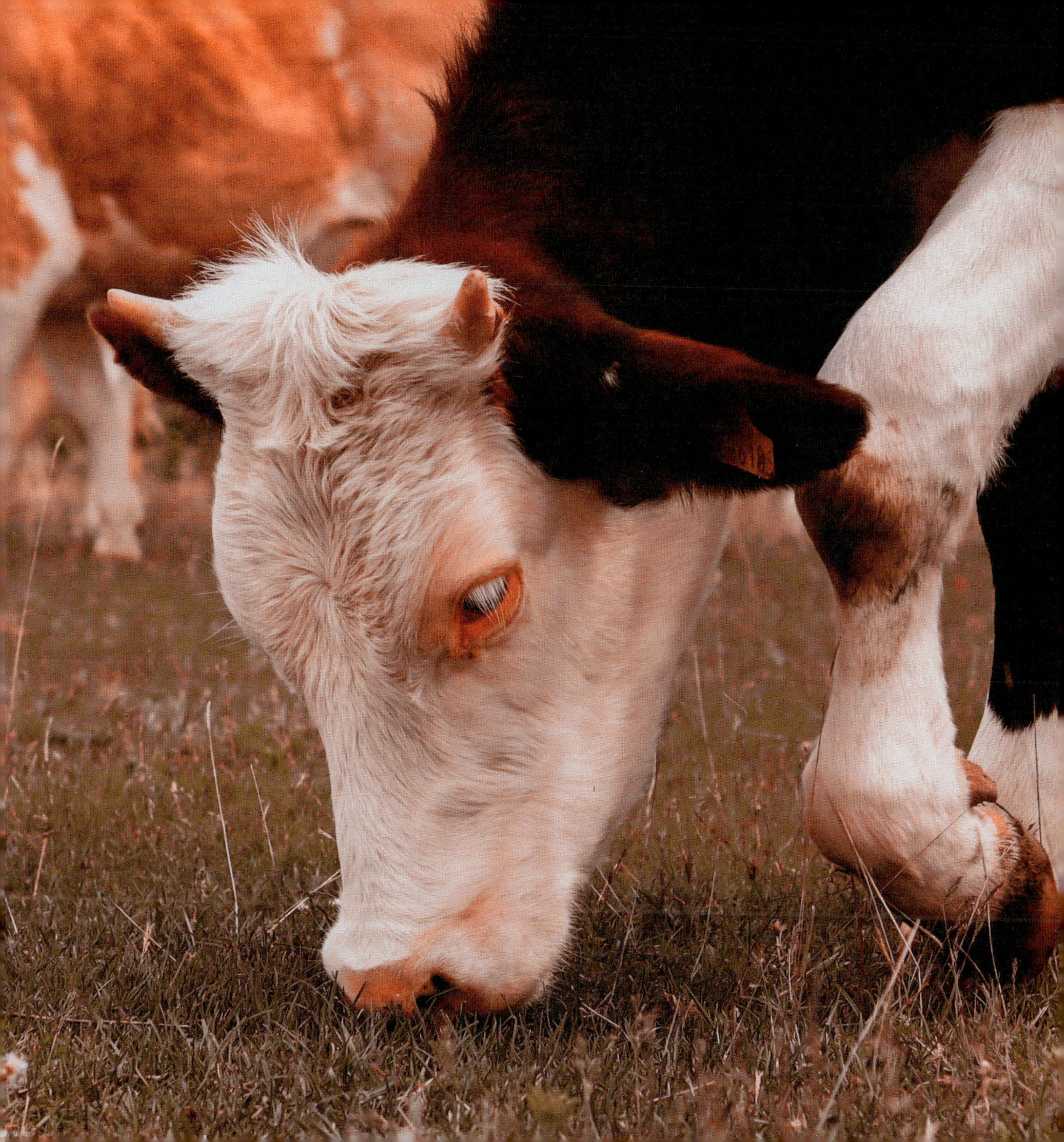

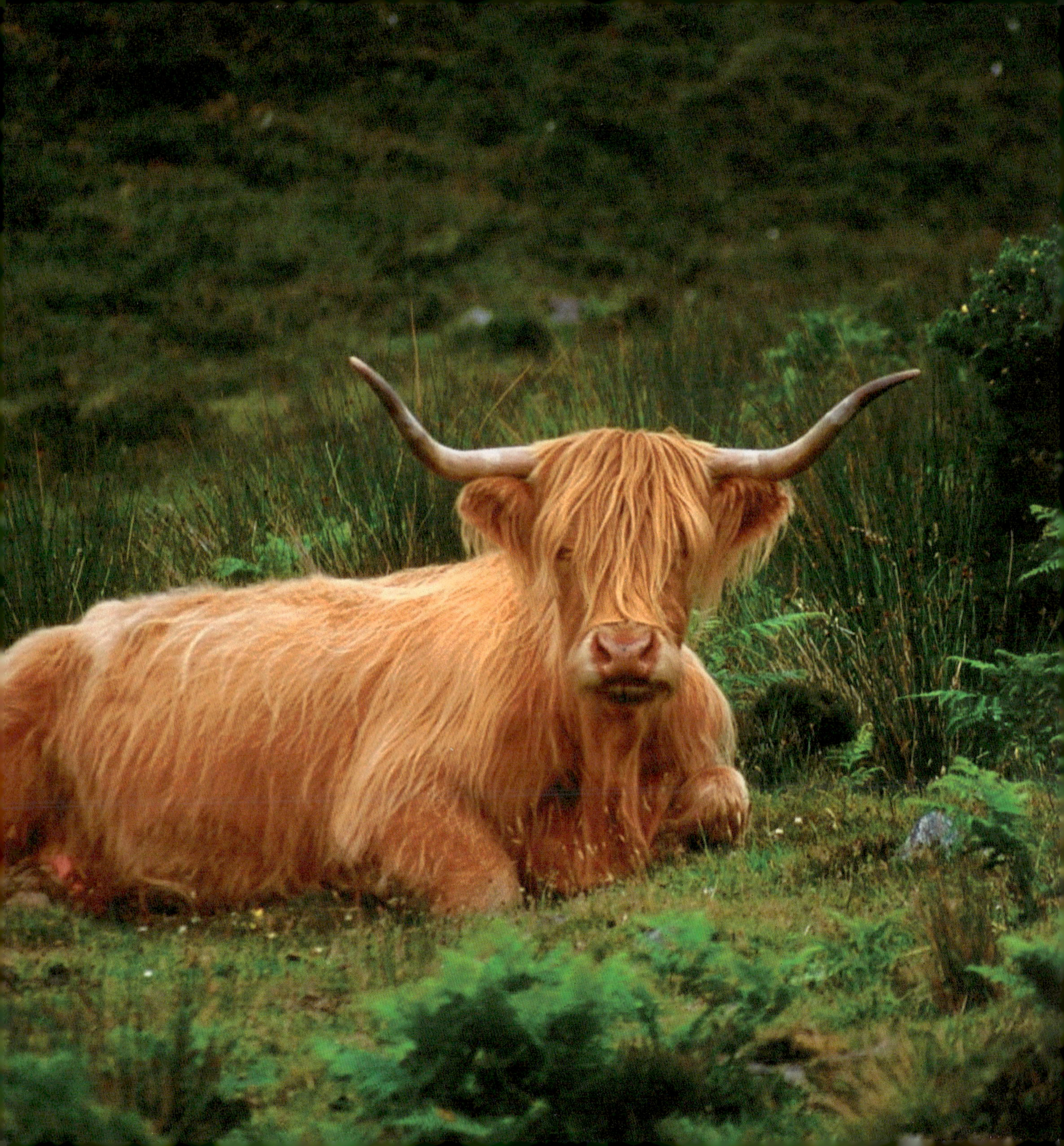

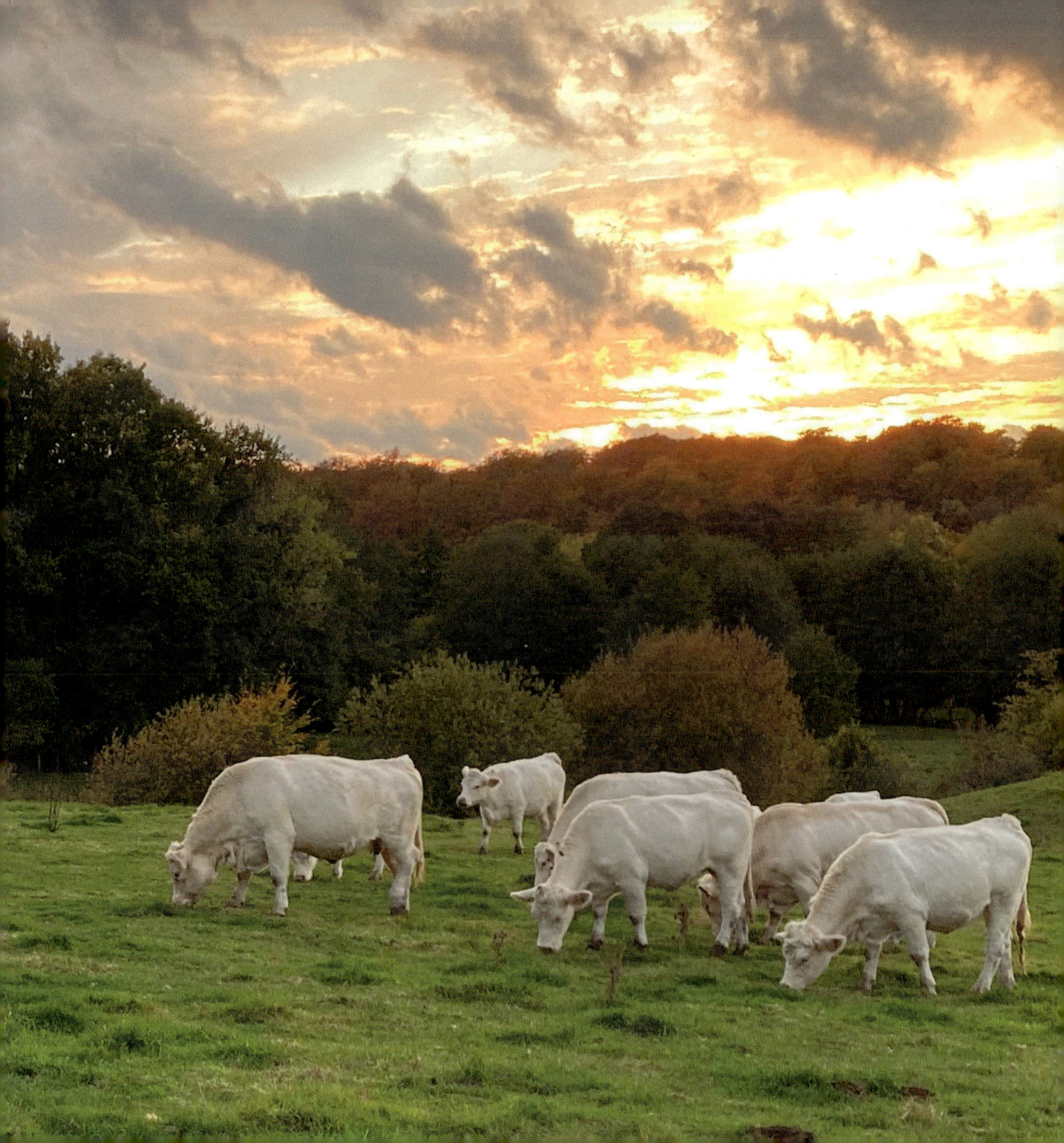

Printed in Great Britain
by Amazon

57959636R00024